John F
D0114054

No Rocking Chair for Me!

NO
Rocking Chair
for Me!

Harold E. Dye

BROADMAN PRESS
Nashville, Tennessee

ISBN: 0-8054-5234-6
4252-34

Library of Congress Catalog Card Number: 75-8325
Dewey Decimal Classification: 301.43
Subject Headings: RETIREMENT / / OLD AGE
Printed in the United States of America

For

Niney

Preface

This book comes at the invitation of Broadman Press who asked the author to write, as a prologue, his actual feelings about his own retirement during the thirty days immediately preceding it. Then, after a full year, the author was to write the other chapters based upon what he had personally experienced—and felt. Therefore, the book is deeply personal.

Much of it is humorous and nostalgic. The pages contain devotion and challenge, with a little offhand advice thrown in. Characters are known by the author and are drawn from the ordinary walks of life.

The author makes no pretense of sociological scholarship. There are no dry statistics, and it does not deal with "programs for the aged," governmental or otherwise. Rather, the book is written conversationally—a retiree to fellow retirees. It is for those who, like the author retired after lives devoted to Christian service combined with the necessities of making a living for those who have come to retirement with reasonably good health and with the financial resources for ordinary needs.

The volume is not all-inclusive. It deals with the *first* stage of retirement—active—only, giving consideration first to the trauma involved, then adjustments, opportunities, and self-realization.

Contents

1. The Rocking Chair   17

2. Elijah's Mantle   25

3. "Thou Bald Head"   39

4. "Give Me That Mountain"   53

5. "My Heart Is Fixed"   69

6. Upside-down World   87

7. "The Woman Thou Gavest"   99

8. Eyes in the Wilderness   109

9. "Come . . . Rest Awhile"   125

10. "I Will Lift Up Mine Eyes"   137

Prologue

January first—New Year's Day. It is shirt-sleeve weather here in California where I live. Although it is winter, some of our roses are in bloom and the grass is green. Just outside my study window the pink camellia is in full bloom, the huge plant reaching up to the eaves of the roof. The azaleas are not yet bedecked with blossoms, but in a couple of months they will splash the side of the house with dark red.

Oranges still cling to the branches of the tree at the back fence, behind the flower garden. They are big, this year— Washington Navels with nary a seed. The tangerine has green balls that will turn first yellow and then orange color. They mingle with the white blossoms which peep out here and there among the leaves as they tremble in the breeze.

From my study window I can see the rock garden and the fish pool with its water lilies. Giant tree ferns form a backdrop to the pool. Rocks from almost every one of the fifty states are built into a miniature mountain behind the pool. Ina and I have gathered the rocks ourselves.

There is the petrified log which we rolled down the real mountain behind Highland Lakes, a discovery that I had made on a deer hunting trip in this rugged area beyond all roads. We had to partially build a path for our four-wheel drive vehicle and then winch the natural-looking section of ancient tree up to where we could load it.

There is the snow-white rock which I dug from the edge of the Worthington Glacier in Alaska, then had to pay extra baggage rates on the plane in order to get it home. A foot-long slab of flint came from the place where my grand-parents lived in the "Little Ozarks" of Oklahoma. Some of my most cherished memories go back to the "blackjack oak" country of the Cherokee Nation.

There is a heavy rock of copper-laden ore which I pried from the wall of a mine near Sierra Blanca, Texas, where my brother-in-law Roy thought he would get rich but instead lost his shirt . . . . The memories themselves are not of rock but are spun out of gossamer threads . . . .

Little waterfalls splash down the miniature mountain at the pressing of a switch in the patio room and floodlights come on simultaneously to make the garden a fairyland.

Would you believe that the giant redwood tree, towering some seventy-five feet in the air and three feet in diameter through its lower trunk, was planted by Ina and me when it was just six inches high? I had simply pulled it up by the roots in a canyon in the Santa Cruz Mountains, ten miles away. That was only twenty years ago.

The fact is that we planted every tree on the lot, the

peach first, then the Santa Rosa plum, a fancy cherry tree bearing five different kinds of cherries, an apricot, an apple, two almonds, three kinds of citrus fruit trees, an avocado—these I can see from my study window now.

When we bought the lot, it was on a dead-end street with acres of cherry trees on that end and acres of prunes across the boulevard from the other end—just one long suburban block. We thought that we were building in the country.

I had the foundation of the house poured, a septic tank built, but all the rest I built with my own hands, from the redwood sills to the cedar shingle roof. It is ranch-styled, sheathed with clear redwood siding. Every stud, every rafter, every joist, is number one dimensional material. I did the plumbing, the electrical wiring—it even tires me now to think of it. Twenty-one years ago we moved into our new house, but I am still building on it here and there. On the back of the house is a glassed-in patio that serves as a sunken dining room. Across one end I built a two-way barbecue and fireplace out of used brick. My study opens out to the patio by sliding glass doors. There are four sets of these six-foot wide doors from house to patio and from the patio to the garden and lawn.

My study is panelled in knotty pine—one inch, foot-wide, solid boards (no plywood!). At one end is a hobby nook where I have my gun cabinet and reloading equipment. There are books everywhere, floor to ceiling except for window space and filing cabinets disguised behind knotty pine cabinets.

This is home.

But how long will it be?

February 1 I shall retire. That is just one month away. Taxes will be sixty dollars a month, utilities (now paid by the church which I serve) will be another fifty. The insurance, the up-keep, and the etceteras will cost an unknown amount. I have very little savings (less than $1,000) from which to draw in an emergency. I do have Social Security, of course, and a small minister's retirement certificate, paying $156 per month. And Medicare can save us from financial disaster (we hope) should the old ticker which is now kicking up fail to the point of lengthy hospitalization. (I am putting my own ailment first in this gloomy "if" because I can still do a man's hard physical labor or, so far as I know, everything I could ever do except, as my doctor says, "eat a heavy meal and then run uphill in a cold wind carrying a suitcase." He also said to give up cigarettes; but since I never smoked in my life, that presented the kind of problem that I am best at solving.) What I am trying to say is that I can still look after my wife in sickness and in health as I promised the preacher nearly a half century ago. That is, I can do it *now*. Tomorrow?

That is, perhaps, the main reason that I am just plain scared. As a man, I feel emasculated. As a pastor (which I have been for forty-six years), I am finished.

When I was young, I could hardly wait for this day. I thought that it would mark the beginning of a sort of earthly heaven. No alarm clocks . . . no pressing schedules to meet . . . time to travel and see the world . . . time to hunt and fish, collect rocks, and make photographs . . . time to spend in my workshop and to fashion pretty things out of wood and metal . . . time to write the books conceived in mind but not yet born on paper . .

the chance to preach now and then without corresponding pastoral responsibilities . . . no more church business meetings with me in the hot seat . . . .

I was young then—and tired.

Now the day is here.

Phooey.

I am old now—and tired.

Or so say the would-be shapers of my destiny.

But before they slap me in the face with a shovel, I have something to say.

Maybe I *am* tired.

Maybe I *am* scared.

But I am also getting mad. I refuse to be buried and forgotten while I am still able to kick up a little dust!

1
The Rocking Chair

Forty years ago I met a strange old man and his amazing rocking chair. I am certain that could I find my way
back into that remote mountain canyon near Cloud-
croft, New Mexico, I would find him again, though he
was at that time more than eighty years old. Old soldiers
like Uncle Zeb never die, and General MacArthur not-
withstanding, they don't even fade away.

I stumbled upon his little homestead wholly by accident. I certainly was not looking for it. I was trailing
a big muley buck through about six inches of new snow
and was bone-tired. My feet were wet, my legs ached,
my ears were nearly frostbitten. Then I saw the cabin.
It was made of logs, chinked with clay. The snow
had melted around the rock chimney of the fireplace,
which was free standing, having long since pulled away
from the walls about four inches. The bare place

on the roof exposed hand-split cedar shakes worn by the rain and snow of half a hundred years. From the chimney curled delicious, beautiful smoke, scented by the aromatic incense of juniper logs.

The buck was forgotten. In those days there were many more. I could probably get one on my way back to camp, six or seven miles away. Right now I wanted to get a sample of that fire. I wanted to wheedle somebody out of a cup of coffee. I wanted to sit down on something more than a snow-covered stump. I opened the rickety gate in the barbed wire fence and was soon standing on the porch of the little cabin. Before I could call out and announce my presence, the front door opened with a bang that sent it back against the wall.

"Come in, come in!" It was more of a command than an invitation. "Front handle's Zeb. There's some as call me 'Uncle Zeb,' though I ain't knowing exactly why."

The old fellow in the doorway was small, wiry; would have weighed about one hundred thirty pounds sopping wet with all his clothes and boots on. His hair, beard, and eyebrows were white as the snow that stretched to the distant peaks. His eyes were alert, alive, black as ebony. They looked out from behind gold-rimmed "specs." He had retrieved the latch on the door by stepping out on the porch. With that clasped in one bony hand, he slapped me on the shoulder with the other and yelled, "Git in there to the fire! You want to freeze me to death on my own door-step?"

The warmth inside the cabin fell on me like a fuzzy wool blanket. I tossed off my water-soaked jacket, leaned my rifle against the doorjamb, and was before the fire in almost one continuous motion. If there is any greater luxury in this old world than blazing logs in a cabin fireplace when the snow lies deep in mountain canyons, I have never discovered it. I toasted my front, then I toasted my back, and in turn, toasted each side. I held up one booted foot until the leather smoked, then held up the other.

Uncle Zeb had sat down slowly in a sturdy cane-bottomed chair to the left of the fireplace. "You were trackin' old 'One Ear,'" he said, "he done come through 'bout an hour ago. I coulda had 'im." He pointed to an ancient Winchester .30-30 leaning against the side of the fireplace. "I trained my sights on 'im just for fun but I already have my meat for the winter. Besides, I kinda like the old cuss. Him and me are somehow kin to one another. Besides, I feel ashamed about old One Ear. I tried a runnin' shot at 'im three years back. Would've been a heart shot, and he'd never have knowed what hit 'im. I like my meat same as most people does, but I don't want to see any animal suffer. That's why, since my eyes ain't so good as they once was, I don't often try for runnin' shots. I guess that old buck musta just zigged where he'd orta zagged. Anyways, I shot his left ear plumb off. I ain't been hungry enough to shoot at 'im since—and I'd have to be powerful hungry to do it."

I began to wonder whether the old man had called me into his cabin for my sake or for One Ear's.

"Hey!" yelled Uncle Zeb, "set down. I ain't used to havin' somebody to shoot the breeze with, and I plumb forgot my manners. Take that chair over there while I pour up a coupla cups of Java." He indicated an amazing rocking chair to my left as he slowly, with creaking joints, got up from his own straight chair.

I started to obey but first looked at the rocking chair
with heightening curiosity. The back and seat were cow-
hide, hair side out. The framework was oak, laboriously
sawn by hand. The rockers, though, caught and held my
attention. How on earth had the old man managed to saw
them?

Uncle Zeb brought two steaming cups of coffee from the
tiny lean-to kitchen. He handed one to me and then creaked
down into his own chair. I had already sunk into the hand-
made rocker. It was one of the most comfortable chairs
that I had ever sat in.

"How do you like that chair?" asked my grizzled host
between sips of blistering coffee.

"Great!" I said, enthusiastically, "I was just wondering
how you managed to cut these rockers."

"With a common handsaw," he said with a twinkle in his
eye. "Now you are fixin' to say it couldn't be done. That
a feller'd have to have a power band saw to do work like
that."

"You took the words right out of my mouth."

Uncle Zeb laughed. "They all say that. I'll admit it had
me stymied for while, but when I gits determined to do
somethin', I do it! I finally got the thing figgered out. I
took me a green one-by-four of oak and put it in the hot
sun with the ends of the board on some big rocks. Then I
heated up some b'iling water and poured it on the middle
of the green board. Then I put about a fifty pound rock in
the middle and two about half that size on either side of
the big one so I could git a even curve. Then I just let ole
Sol do his stuff. After the board was curved just right, I
took my handsaw and sawed right down the center of it,

end to end, and there was my rockers," he chuckled.

"It sure is a comfortable chair," I said, "why weren't you sitting in it?"

"I didn't build it fer *me* to set in," the old man said. "I built it fer m' company. A contraption like that is only good fer old people—or maybe tenderfoot deer hunters," he hastily added, unflatteringly, but without sarcasm.

His answer interested me, and I put the question forming in my mind. "Are you afraid that if you sit down in this comfortable rocking chair, you might rock yourself to sleep and miss something?" I thought that I would pay him back for that "tenderfoot" crack.

"That is 'xactly what I do mean," the old fellow said, "I ain't goin' to sit in no rockin' chair and rock my life away. I got work to do. Once a feller takes to his rockin' chair, he is done."

The rocking chair suddenly became uncomfortable to me. I stood up. I had finally realized that unless I hit the trail soon, I would be long after dark getting back to camp. I told my grizzled host good-bye, put on my still-damp hunting jacket, picked up my rifle, and headed out into the chill of the high mountain air.

All the way down the trail the vision of the old man and his rocking chair kept intruding into my other thoughts. I did only casual hunting. I had mental meat for my mind to chew on. Finally, as darkness began to settle over the canyon, I saw the welcome light of my own campfire, and the shadowy forms of my two hunting partners as they moved around it. I gave them my famous yodel, and it was answered by the staccato barking of an outraged coyote on some far-off slope.

Forty winters have now come and gone since that afternoon and night, but a picture still lingers with me . . . .
In my mind's eye I see a grizzled, resolute old man and
his homemade rocking chair in which he would not "set"
for fear of losing life itself.

I am not trying to start an ARM (antirocking chair movement). There are so many bureaucratic abecedarian desig-
nations now and so many protesters with their signs that
we'll soon have to invent an alphabet with more letters or
stop agitating. I heard of another one the other day for us
oldsters: SOGPIP—silly old grandma with pictures in her
purse. No; I am not trying to start any movement. Perhaps
I am trying to *stop* one, I don't know. I have convinced
myself that my old friend of the long ago had made a good
point: once you sit down in the comfort of a rocking
chair, it is hard to get up. While old Zeb had his own personal reason for not taking to idleness—he lived, for the
most part, secluded from the lives of his fellowmen—I have
an even better reason. While I rocked my life away, the
world would go on needing some little something that I
could give to make it a better place for those who follow
me.

You can rock all day long as hard as you like in your
easy rocking chair but when the night comes, how far have
you been? I have heard of wheelchair races—and I glory
in such zest for living—but who ever heard of a rocking
chair race?

In the interest of accuracy, I looked up "rocking chair"
in the index of *Guinness Book of World Records,* and I followed through to a description of a "Rockathon" in which
a certain Ralph Weir, aged 55, of Truro, Nova Scotia,

Canada, laid claim to fame by rocking 108 hours on September 1-5, 1960. Maybe that makes some kind of sense but my point is that poor old Ralph rocked all those days and gained not one foot of ground. All he did was to wear a groove in the floor and a blister on his backside, and when they helped him out of the chair, he had been nowhere at all.

I prefer Uncle Zeb's attitude: "That ain't fer me."

2
Elijah's Mantle

"Old Elijah stood by his rocket ship waiting for the countdown," the little boy said. "Off there behind a cloud somewhere the angel said: 'Minus thirty seconds and counting.' Elijah whipped off his earth coat and threw it on the ground. He got into his space suit and climbed up the ladder into the rocket ship and just then the angel yelled, 'Blast off!' And up went that old rocket and the fire shot out of its tail—and zaroom! It was gone! Then Elisha ran over and picked up Elijah's coat and put it on."

I reluctantly interrupted this exciting narrative. Evidently this kid knew something that I didn't so I asked, "Why did Elijah have to go to heaven in the chariot of fire, or rocket, or whatever you call it?" You see, the Bible does not say why.

The little fellow looked at me with more than a trace of condescension. "Elijah got too old. God can't use old

people anymore here on earth. I know cause my
grandpa said so. God said, 'Elijah, I'm sending a spaceship
down to you and you can give your earth coat to Elisha
and he will do your work after that. Elisha sounds like
Elijah only he wasn't.''

"How do you think Elijah felt about all that?" I asked,
curiously. The Bible doesn't say anything about that,
either. Evidently this kid had a straight wire out and could
get classified information direct.

His blue eyes widened. Even his freckles seemed to grow
appreciably larger. Then came the answer. It was not top
drawer stuff but his own thinking: "Elijah got old, like I
said, and I don't really think he wanted to go, but old folks
has got no choice, my grandpa said. He probably didn't
think that Elisha could do as good a job as he had done.
Old folks never think us young ones can do much."

I looked at that eight-year-old. I could tell by his eyes
that he was ready to take on all comers. I should have
stopped when I was even.

"Surely you don't think that Elisha was just eight years
old, as you are. It seems to me that I read that he was
bald-headed."

The kid never batted a blue eye. "So's Yul Brynner," he
said," and he's not old." I wondered, dully, how Yul
Brynner got mixed up in that Bible story. I was sure, then,
that I had missed something, but the kid was talking and I
did not want to miss one word of it. "Anyway, Elisha
must have been a whole lot younger than Elijah was. That's
why Elijah gave him his coat. It was a brand-new coat, and
Elijah wouldn't have time to wear it out."

"Which would you have rather been, Elijah or Elisha, if

you could have had your choice?" I asked, out of simple
curiosity.

Again that look of condescension. "Elijah, of course.
He got to ride in that rocket ship." Then the kid surprised
me out of my wits and closed my mouth for certain. "You
know," he said, "Elijah got to come back. I read about it
in the New Testament in Sunday School class. And you
know what?"

I waited breathlessly for his answer, but I was really beginning to hate him.

"He found that the world was getting along all right without him. In fact it was getting along better, and do you
know why? Jesus was there."

* * *

When I retired from the pulpit of Baptist Temple, San
Jose, California, after a service of twenty-two years, guess
what! The church promptly called a theological whiz kid
still enrolled in Golden Gate Baptist Seminary to take my
place. He was just twenty-four years old. Why, since I
had been ordained at the age of nineteen, I had been
preaching twice as long as that twirp had been in the world!

My wife and I (lacking a chariot of fire and horses of fire
from heaven) did the next best thing. We hooked our little
trailer to our four-wheel-drive vehicle and headed off to
parts unknown for a stay of several months—until the
"honeymoon" of the new pastor and church was over.
Finally we crept back home.

The very first Sunday we were back, I watched the *boy*
who had taken my place perform a baptismal service. I
could not believe my eyes. He did it all backward. Now it
so happens that I built that baptistry myself in the long ago.

In fact, it was one of the first fiberglassed baptismal pools ever built. I reasoned that, if a fellow could fiberglass a boat to keep water out, he could fiberglass a big box to keep water in. I built that baptistry to be used in just one way: the candidate was to be baptized from left to right.

Well, anyway, this kid pastor came down the baptistry steps all dressed up in *my* rubber pants and robe. He reached up and took a pretty teenaged girl by the hand and helped her down the steps. He lifted his hand and repeated the old familiar formula and then proceeded to lay the candidate down from the *right* side instead of from the left. How do you like that?

As far as I was concerned, the whole procedure was sacrilegious. It was downright unbiblical. Anybody who knows anything at all about Palestine knows that the Jordan River runs from left to right, or north to south (when it is not running east and west like a crooked snake). Now, as I said, the Jordan runs from left to right. In fact, all rivers run from left to right. Notice the next time. If the river where you are standing seems to violate this rule, just cross over to the other side and see what happens. That is because it is easier to baptize from left to right. Maybe that is why the Bible describes the place where John was baptizing as Bethabara (house of the ford). This was not a garage for a certain automobile, nor was it the home of a certain President of the United States. It was a place where John could cross over to the other side—a ford.

Something else. Any of us old-timers can tell any kid preacher (if he will listen) that when you baptize in a stream you baptize the candidate with the candidate-person's head upstream. The reason is obvious; otherwise

you might drown the candidate. The baptistry in the
church building is probably unscriptural, but we'll let that
pass in favor of saying that the baptistry *symbolizes* the
river Jordan which runs from left to right. Do you follow
my reasoning? But these kid preachers never heard of baptizing a candidateperson with his (her) head upstream. The
seminaries don't say a thing about that anymore. Instead,
they teach such things as "ministerial ethics." Totally
useless. I served as pastor nearly half a century without
any ethics at all.

Finally this—boy —got up to preach, and his very first
words turned me off. Although the auditorium is small,
he had two microphones before him. They are connected
to an amplifier with dials all lighted up like the console of
a 747. Then from the forty-watt amplifier the sound is
piped to two big speakers tucked high against the beamed
ceiling. I thought: what's the matter with this kid? Is he
so lazy that he can't talk? Are his lungs so weak that he
can't be heard sixty feet? I can prove that when I preached
I woke up the people in an apartment building four blocks
away. Again, I'll only hint at infidelity to the Bible. Peter
didn't need any electronic assistance to preach on the day
of Pentecost. He preached in every tongue there was without benefit of microphone. If you ask me, the ministry
nowadays is getting too soft.

I have to admit that the young fellow looked nice in the
pulpit—except for one thing: he had hair. Now I really
believe that a man looks far more dignified and intellectual
if he, like me, is partially bald. It somehow adds to his
ministerial demeanor. I also have to admit—grudgingly—
that, when the young man preached, he captured and held

my interest. If I could only be sure that he would never read this (I would not want to give him a swelled head), I would have to confess that the sermon itself was fundamental, scriptural, Baptistic, well-prepared, and timely. But why all that gadgetry? See my point? There are wrong ways to do a right thing.

Something else I soon found out. This boy preacher set up a bunch of committees. The church looks like a democratic congress. He's got a committee for this and a committee for that and a committee on committees to check up on all the rest. He calls it "delegated responsibility." Phooey! As far as I am concerned, that is all a ministerial cop-out.

I always figured that a church called me ("hired" might follow my thinking better) to do all the work that needed to be done. I suppose that this is a throwback to my newspaper days. When I accepted my first half-time church back in New Mexico, I supported my family by publishing a weekly newspaper. Come to think of it, I was just twenty-two then—but I was very mature. One day I received a letter inviting me to a big publishers' convention in Denver, Colorado. The invitation said for me to bring my managing editor, city editor, state and national editors, society editor, sports editor, all reporters, and others on the editorial staff. Even the typesetters, the pressmen, mailers—the whole works were invited to attend, RSVP. I wrote back, "I'll be there."

I carried this same system over into my church work. I never thought that I could trust ordinary church members to win souls, to visit the sick and troubled, and if I could have had my way there would have been just one big Sun-

day School class for all ages—with me teaching it. After
all, hadn't I studied much more about all these things?

Well, as I was saying—or did I admit so much?—I have
a theory. If a pastor expects to stay in any church a long
time, he has to make himself indispensable. He certainly
has to earn his wages or the same will cease and desist, and
he'll get pretty hungry. I am a pretty good jack-of-all-
trades. I am a fairly proficient carpenter, electrician,
plumber, cabinetmaker—you name it. I can do it. Do you
think that Baptist Temple had to call in any of the journey-
men dudes suggested above to fix the toilets or do anything
like that? Don't be silly.

I went about making myself indispensable. After all,
what church or business can afford to fire a man whom
they cannot do without? I had things so well worked out
that the church could hardly operate without me.

Take the time I broke my ankle in five places. I was
coming down the shale slope of a mountain in the High
Sierras of California, up on Sonora Pass. I have always
believed myself to be an exceptionally good mountain-
down-comer so I was leaping along like an alpine billy goat
when I stepped on a rock which was not, as we say poet-
ically, "anchored to the eternities." Skipping the painful
details (my ankle still has five long screws in it, and it
aches everytime I think of it at all), after I landed on the
rocks, I landed in a hospital some sixty miles away in the
little town of Sonora. I had been there just two days—two
days, mind you!—when I received a telegram from a deacon
in San Jose:

Harold E. Dye
Community Hospital, Sonora, California

HOW DO YOU GET THE FRONT DOOR UNLOCKED STOP.

There is quite a trick to unlocking that front door. In the first place, the lower hinge lets it sag. You know, of course, that in hanging a door you always leave seven inches at the top and eleven inches at the bottom when you put on the hinges (that is, you know it if you are not some young squirt just out of the seminary). Well, the front door of Baptist Temple (unless they hired a carpenter to fix it) is not that way. It has always sagged, and the bottom drags on the concrete of the porch. It may be that the concrete itself has shifted a little. At any rate, you have to grasp the door firmly and lift it as you swing it in position. It won't lock from the outside at all. That's why the deacon got into trouble. He tried to lock it from the outside and got his key broken off in the lock. It is really very simple. You just have to lock it from the inside, *always.*

Then I had gone off on the trip and had left the water in the baptistry after a baptizing Sunday night. I always filled the baptistry myself because I was afraid that someone else, being absent-minded, might let the water run over. As I say, I forgot to drain the tank.

Now, in order for you to understand what followed, I should tell you that the vent pipe was stopped up. The deacon did not know that so he pulled the overflow pipe out of its seat and the water began to drain out, but it went too fast. After a few minutes the water was coming out in the kitchen sink and also in the drinking fountain in the hall. It ran over from the sink in the kitchen and ruined the floor tile, and it overflowed the bowl of the drinking fountain. I had always just pulled the pipe up a

little way so the water went out slowly. You see, I was
the only one who knew those things, and I intentionally
kept it that way. That is why I was so important.

And did that deacon have trouble trying to lock up all
the back doors! On some of them you had to twist the
locking button until it was straight up. But on others you
turned it to where it was horizontal. See what I mean? If
you work at it, you can. I understood about such things
in connection with our church. That is why I was missed
so much when I was out breaking my bones.

It was a good thing that it was summer, and they did
not need any heat. Some of the children would have
turned into icicles. One Sunday School room was heated
by an old-fashioned gas stove (before a central heating
system was put in the educational building). You turned
off the old stove with a claw hammer. What's that? You
say you never heard of such a thing? Probably not, because being smart about such things, I invented the process. I always put the claw hammer on the little shaft
where the turner-offer used to be and caught the claw on
the squared shank. Then one turn to the left and whammo!
The stove was in business.

Now let me tell you about the lights! Did that deacon
have fun with them! Somebody heard him yell: "How
do you get this bank of lights off?" You see, we had a
relay system on the lights actuated by a button on a dial
like on your radio, and it worked fine most of the time;
but if it didn't you had to go to the breaker box in the
hallway and jiggle breaker number 24. It was just that
simple, but I was the only one who knew how to do all
those things. It always made me feel pretty smart because

there were six licensed electricians in the church. There were also several carpenters in the congregation, as well as two plumbers, but I usually took care of such matters.

After all, I had more time than they had. I could always leave off a hospital call to unstop a sink. Anyway, they were busy men, and if the church did have to call a plumber, remember that a plumber gets just twice as much pay as a preacher does. The church was not broke. It had the money for all these things without any strain, but you see, I was using the old noodle, that is, until the deacons called me on the carpet and told me . . . aw skip it! They didn't seem to appreciate some of the things I was doing "in place of."

But let me tell you one more example (I've got lots of them!). I should mention how much trouble they had with the mimeograph machine when they tried to put out the bulletin. It takes twenty-two sheets of scrap paper as a cushion on the feed tray to get the corrugated rubber feet to push the new stock through. I did those things automatically. I didn't even have to think about it. It took them four hours to do what I always did in fifteen minutes.

That was the reason I was able to stay at Baptist Temple twenty-two years.

I wonder how long this new preacher will last. My advice to him (which he hasn't asked me for) would be to forget all about that "delegated responsibility" stuff and make himself indispensable.

Now, laying aside the lighthearted banter and getting down to the "nitty-gritty" of the matter, is not that the

way most of us feel about the one who had been chosen
to take our place? Just about every single thing he (or she)
does is wrong. It is not the way we would have acted under
the same circumstances. Of course not! I am I; you are
you; he is he; and she is she. And that's not only the way
it has to be—it is the way it should be.

No one of us is indispensable. On the other hand, we
are expendable. As the little boy who introduced this
chapter said about Elijah, the world rocked along all right—
even better—without him in it. That is strong medicine
for us to take, but the sooner we take it the sooner we'll
get well from the disease of frustration. Someone can and
no doubt will take our place, and just might do a better
job. That pill is particularly hard to swallow, but swallow
it we must—and not wash it down with tears of self-pity.

The more dedicated we were to the work which we were
doing, the more sensitive we are to the one who followed
us. The more, too, we are inclined to major on his defi-
ciencies and to magnify the inconsequential. Perhaps it
would help us to be more charitable if we looked backward
into our own experiences and remembered at least some of
our own mistakes. We made them, you know. What is
more, people were usually kind to us when we did.

During the early years of my ministry I said things in
the pulpit which I would never repeat in that sacred place
today; not because I now lack the courage to do so, but I
have better sense. Remember that the best teacher you
ever had was your own experience, and that did not come
to you overnight. You only learned to walk by falling
down. Someone was extremely patient with me; someone
was patient with you. The very least that we can do is to

repay that debt by being patient with that one who put on our moccasins to try to walk our twisted trail.

This time of retirement has put a deep hurt in the heart of each of us. Psychologists rate that hurt at half that of the loss of a lifelong mate. That is to say, if the loss of wife or husband rates 100 on the psychometric scale, the permanent loss of a job through forced retirement rates 50. This shows how serious is the adjustment that the average one of us must make. It is never easy.

A father works all of his adult life building up a business. He has studied the market, has mastered economics, has supplied a need. He has been eminently successful in his enterprise. Then comes the day when he has to hand that business over to his son. The question is: can he really do so? Can he adopt a "hands off" policy? Can he give to the son whom he loves that son's right to personhood? If the answer to all three questions is not positive, the father can doom the business into which he has poured his life's blood; he can doom the son of his love to failure; he can doom his own final years to wreckage.

There are many who think that the present governor of California is a "strange sort of duck." I'll take the Fifth Amendment on that.

The newspapers reported that Edmund G. Brown, Jr., who studied for the Roman Catholic priesthood, spent two days immediately following his election victory practicing "zazen," the technique of sitting meditation used by the Zen sect of Buddhism.

I did not vote for Junior, not because he had studied for the priesthood, not because he could "zen" himself into some transcendental trance, but because he was the

son of his father. Two terms ago Edmund G. Brown, Sr.,
was governor, and I lived under his administration. I
neither liked him nor it. Then when Edmund G. Brown,
Jr., ran for the highest office in the state, I was sure that
he would be a carbon copy of his father.

Right off the reel, though, young Governor Jerry Brown
cut squarely across his dad's ideas and arguments. Edmund
G. Brown, Sr., learned, if he had to learn it, that this was
a whole new ball game, and he was not the pitcher. I liked
that!

It is too early to know what kind of Governor Edmund
Brown, Jr., will make, or whether or not "zazen" is the
ultimate in political secret weapons, so I reserve judgment
at this point.

I watched a TV reporter interview Mrs. Edmund G.
Brown, Sr. You see, she was the Governor's wife. She is
now the Governor's mother. She is caught in the squeeze.
If I remember correctly when the reporter asked her if she
found her position a difficult one, she just smiled and
shrugged.

One thing I know: Jerry Brown will make a much better
governor if he makes his dad, Brown, Senior, keep out of
his way. So far, he has.

I am even more convinced that James Bush will make
a better pastor of Baptist Temple if I just keep out of his
way. That I shall do.

The church which I left at age sixty-seven is in the
strong capable hands of a mature young man regardless of
his chronological age. It is doing well. My wife and I are
happy members of it. I have offered no advice to the
youthful pastor, have never usurped any of his pastoral

duties, have no place of leadership, nor will I accept one. The pastor has only my encouragement, my prayers, my love, and none of my envy.

It is common knowledge that many a church has been wrecked by a former pastor who could not keep his hands off. This is especially true of churches where the pastor has been of long tenure. The problem is compounded, of course, if the former pastor stays on as a member of the church. This is not to say that he should not. I did. It is to say, however, that if he is going to hinder the ministry of the man of God called to take his place, he had better remove himself as far from the scene as possible and keep himself incommunicado.

We *can* go home again, if we behave.

3
"Thou Bald Head"

I had always thought that the passage about Elisha's bald head, the children, and the bears in the Bible was the classic horror story of all time. It honestly worried me during the first twenty years of my ministry.

The King James Version gives a very graphic picture of the little brats who followed the prophet, yelling at the top of their leather lungs: "Go up, thou bald head; go up, thou bald head." Can't you just see them? Can't you hear them?

That poor old man was going along, minding his own business, looking prophetic, and these miniature maniacs took after him. They touched him on a most sensitive spot. He had probably used ten gallons of Baruch's Hair Restorer to stop the infernal fallout, and there were these yowling kids throwing live coals of fire into his boiling torment. Had I been Elisha, I'd have kicked them all the way back to Bethel and ten miles the other side. The old bald head, being a nonviolent man—up to a point—turned around and cursed them in the name of the Lord.

Here is where I used to shudder and close my Bible: two big she-bears came galloping out of the woods and "tare forty and two of them"—admittedly too many for the toe of Elisha's foot, especially when he was wearing sandals—notoriously poor equipment for kicking tough kids.

I used to believe that the old she-bears ate the little children up. I didn't like that idea then; I am not so sure about it now. When I had hair, I could not conceive of such cruelty to little kids, who, after all, were just having a little fun.

Then one day I confessed my abhorrence of the story to my good friend, Bill Bolton, who afterwards became a noted chaplain in World War II. Bill, a better scholar than I, said, "The Bible doesn't say that the bears ate the children up. It just says that they 'tare' them. That meant that the bears could just have scratched the kids."

I was so relieved that I could have kissed Bill, but that would have gotten me stomped. I notice that *The New English Bible* simply says that the bears "mauled" the kids. Furthermore (women's libbers take note), this version of the Bible says that all the mean little kids were boys.

Anyway, as they used to say when I was a mean little kid in the Ozarks, that "broke them little skunks from suckin' eggs."

But Elisha still went on getting balder and balder. It is a frightening thing to a man when he begins to lose his hair. I suppose that it is to a woman, also if, or when, she she does so, except who would know it? It is fashionable

for her to adorn herself with a wig. Even if she has her
natural hair, as luxuriant as the raven tresses of the Queen
of Sheba, she is likely to cover it up with a blonde dandruff-
proof, acrylic masterpiece. Not so with a man.

Of course a man can wear a wig, too. But it can be hazardous. It can also be embarrassing. My pastor friend, Guy
Bradley, started to baptize one of the wig-wearing gentlemen, and he told the man to remove his wig. The candidate
refused. "It's all right; it won't come off." But it did!
Guy says that he lowered the man into the water and to
his horror, the wig floated off. He grabbed the hairpiece,
slammed it down on the man's head—but got it on side-
ways. Fortunately the attendant drew the curtains fast.

Dr. A. L. Aulick, the internationally-known Bible scholar,
the ultimate personification of ministerial dignity, is now
deceased. He told me many years ago about receiving a
young mother into the fellowship of the church. The little
mother had walked down the aisle carrying her two-year-
old baby girl. Dr. Aulick lifted the little girl up in his arms
and just as he did so, the little one reached up and jerked
the doctor's wig from his head. He was the only one in
the auditorium who did not think *that* funny.

I used to have more hair than the "king of the hippies."
I have treasured pictures to prove it. Then in my fifties
my hair began to leave home. I worried about it. I spent
a lot of money trying to keep it fastened to my scalp.
Then my brother, John, told me that he heard of a fellow
who had cured his scalp of its propensity for shedding. It
seems that this bird bent over early every morning and
rubbed salt on his head—all over the bald spot. He rubbed
until the bald spot was a deep red, like a turkey's wattle—

always rubbing in the good old sodium chloride. Pretty soon the hair was coming back in. First it was just a light fuzz like that on a peach. Then it was a thicker and deeper fuzz like that on a new-hatched chick, and finally, he looked like Rudolph Valentino used to look.

That sounded reasonable to me, and I tried it. Morning after morning I tried that ritual in the bathroom. Then one morning my wife unexpectedly opened the door and there I was all bent over, diligently rubbing salt on my scalp. She kicked me clear into the bathtub. She said that she just couldn't resist it. It was only then that I decided to give up, and you know what? My hair stopped falling out. Honest. Maybe there is something to this salt treatment after all. If you are a man and reading this, take my advice and keep the bathroom door locked if you try it

The whole point of this is, of course, that hair is the symbol of youth. I do not need to tell you, fellow retiree, either man or woman, that we live in a youth-oriented society. Senator Percy has a book called *Growing Old in the Country of the Young.* It costs $7.95 and I couldn't afford it so I walked down to the neighborhood bookstore and read snatches of it from time to time. The book, coming from a United States Senator, may have some political overtones. As I pilfered, mentally, parts of the volume, I felt that the title was more interesting than the content. This is not to downgrade the book; it just did not suit my own needs. It aggravated my own antipathies, so to speak, and they are already aggravated enough as it is. I believe that Senator Percy still has his own hair. This should disqualify him from writing such a book.

If I recall the earth-shaking matter correctly, it was Senator Proxmire and not Senator Percy who had his hair transplanted one hair at a time. Good grief!—as Charlie Brown would say—what a cost! The newspapers reported than an unforgettable West Coast singer, Frank—what's his name?—Oh, well, he had his hair transplanted at a cost of $35 per individual follicle. I might have tried that except at the quoted price I still am a pretty wealthy man—hair-wise. Especially on my chest.

Anyway, it is this aging process, in whatever form it takes, that puts ants in my psychological pants.

Some doctor of philosophy has said, "Halitosis is better than no breath at all." Another erudite gentleman staggered to the lectern and delivered himself of his soul-stirring statement, "I don't mind getting old," he quavered, "when I consider the alternative." Like the Ethiopian in the Bible who could not change his skin, neither can you or I stop our aging process.

When I was in St. Augustine, Florida, I drank at Ponce de Leon's Fountain of Youth, but my hair kept falling out, my teeth kept coming out, my eyes kept right on growing weaker, and my joints kept right on growing creakier. The Fountain of Youth did not do one blooming thing for me. As I recall the old lion, Ponce himself, was soon pushing up daisies.

So, friends, we cannot stop the physiological aging process. We may slow it down a bit by getting the proper exercise, eating the right kinds of food and not too much of it!— and by other methods, but old Tempus will just go on fugiting along.

While we cannot stop the physiological sequence of time,

we *can* stop its psychological march through our minds and
souls. All of us know persons who are in their eighties and
nineties who are younger in spirit and in mind than are
some others in their forties. Cliché or not, it is still true:
You are just as old as you feel." Perhaps a better version
is, "You are as old as you think you are." The Bible says,
"For as he thinketh in his heart, so is he." This can apply
to something more than morals.

I am not a gerontologist (I have never even seen one),
but I do have some opinions based upon my observations
and much reading. One of my opinions is this: *we are old
when we quit learning. Conversely, we are young in pro-
portion to our quest for knowledge.*

Our church, though not large, has a splendid library.
Situated just off the foyer, the room is panelled in walnut
with harmonizing shelves and furniture. A rich-looking,
deep-pile rug covers the floor. Tasteful pictures hang here
and there. Hundreds of good books line the shelves. Visual
aid films are neatly catalogued and stored.

Presiding over the library is Sue House. She is a trained
librarian, a graduate of Samford University, in Birmingham,
Alabama. She, more than anyone else, is responsible for
the effectiveness of the church library in the lives of our
members.

I asked Sue this question, "Who checks out the most
books?" Her answer was, "Women of the T.E.L. Class."
This is a class for the oldest women in the church. Most
of them are widows, living alone. Our librarian singled out
Mrs. Ethel Pope as an example. Mrs. Pope is ninety-one.
She has read more of the library books than has anyone
else. Most of the volumes which she has read are what

young people would call "deep." They are. They cannot
be read without concentration. A few are fiction; most are
factual. The last book which she checked out (just last
Sunday) was Arthur Flake's helpful little treatise, *Life at
Eighty—As I See It*. It is no longer in print but came as
my gift to the church from my own bookshelves.

Any Sunday morning Mrs. Pope and the teacher of the
T.E.L. Class, Mrs. Maxine Lund, a sixty-six-year-old widow,
can be seen walking down the sidewalk to the church building. They live in separate apartments in a big complex two
blocks away. Each of these spry little ladies has, in addition
to her Bible, a volume from the church library—every Sunday. Mrs. Pope is also an artist with a crochet needle, and
in addition to this, finds another way to express her vital
personality: She makes pretty rag dolls for needy children.
Old? Call her that and get ready to duck her swinging hand-
bag.

Admittedly, Mrs. Pope has an advantage. At ninety-one,
she reads without glasses. She reads, though, because she
still wants to learn. She still wants to serve. She still is interested in all that takes place around her, but that interest
extends across the earth. Come to think of it, Mrs. Pope
and I, together, watched the first landing on the moon, so
her interests go beyond the earth, to outer space and to
heaven, itself. That's why she is still young at ninety-one.
When I told her about this book, she said, "I can hardly wait
to read it." She will be ninety-two by the time it sees print!

My memory of Mrs. Pope and her excitement at the moon
landing leads to another observation: *we are old when we
become inflexible toward change.* I heard a gray-haired man
teaching an older men's Bible class say, just three years

before it happened, "The day a man steps on the moon, I'll throw my Bible away." By the time those boys took that "giant step for mankind," the Sunday School teacher had moved to another town. I hope that he did not throw the Book away before he heard that memorable Christmas broadcast from the vicinity of the moon in 1968:

> " 'In the beginning God created the heaven and the earth. And the earth was without form and void; and darkness was upon the face of the deep . . . . And God saw that it was good . . . . ' And from the crew of Apollo 8, we close with good night, good luck, and a Merry Christmas. And God bless all of you, all of you on the good Earth."

Frank Borman, James Lovell, and William Anders had not thrown *their* Bible away.

Neither did Neil Armstrong seven months later. When he took his first steps on the moon, he did not walk away from God.

All the time that lunar module was descending, Mrs. Pope was praying, "Dear God, please take care of those young men."

This leads to my third observation: *We are old when we cease to be interested in others.* We can convince ourselves that no one cares about us; why should we care about them?

Many older people take this attitude. They remove themselves from circulation and retire into the cubicles of their own shriveled hearts. Go there, dear friend, and you will be left there!

The fact is, at any stage of life, others care about us as we care about them. One of the youngest men I ever met was eighty-two years old. He was Asbel S. Petrey, pioneer preacher in the Cumberland Mountains for half a century. At the request of the Southern Baptist Home Mission Board, I flew to Kentucky from my home in New Mexico to find Brother Petrey and write his life story for a book on missions. The book was subsequently published under the title, *The Prophet of Little Cane Creek.* Since the book has long since gone out of print, I quote a part of it:

"Howdy, Brother Petrey." The words were followed by a huge, translucent bubble which grew and grew until it almost covered the tiny, freckled face. Brother Petrey watched the bubble in fascination until it finally burst.

"Civilization," he murmured, "has finally arrived in the mountain country." Then to the smiling face before him, he said, "Howdy, Johnny. How's your mother? Did she ever get over those sick spells? And how about your daddy, Jim? Did he go back to work at the mine?"

"Pop's still on strike. He says he's goin' to git justice iffen we all starve to death. Ain't it fierce what these mine owners will do to make a few cents a ton more on coal? But, say, Pop's mine's gittin' a new steel tipple. He 'most wishes he was back at work."

"Listen to me a minute, Johnny. I have been preaching ever since the Harlan Miner's War that there were two sides to that question. Don't go blaming the mine operators until you know their side, too. And I hope the dispute will soon be settled. These times it is hard enough to make a living if you work every day. Now, how about your mother?"

"I meant to tell you about her," said Johnny, "but

we men folks have our problems, too."

I almost laughed at his eight-year-old earnest face.

"Mom is gittin' all right. You see, she is carrying another baby."

"Well, good-bye, Johnny," Brother Petrey said.

We took a few steps down the sidewalk in silence.

"Sometimes I wonder whether our problem in the mountains is one of ignorance or because the wrong people know too much. What right does an eight-year-old kid have to talk like that? Children mature entirely too rapidly when eight or more are raised in a one-room shack." Brother Petrey's face was grave.

"Howdy, preacher." A tall, well-dressed banker touched his straw hat in salute and hurried on.

"That's one of my boys from the Institute. He got all his education there . . . " (Hazard Baptist Institute was started by Petrey).

"Howdy, preacher." This time the speaker stopped. He was an insurance man. He, too, was well-dressed, prosperous looking. I had met him previously at a luncheon.

"Better watch that New Mexican," he jokingly warned his old friend. "He looks dangerous."

"I like dangerous people, Tom. But I don't think he carries a gun, except on his tie clasp. Is Bill about ready for school? Say, he is going off to college, isn't he?"

"Howdy, Preacher."

"Howdy, Sheriff. How's the strong arm of the law?"

"I'm out trying to get them to nominate somebody

else in the primary Saturday."

Hazard was a busy place that morning. A constant
stream of cars nosed along its main street, bumper to
bumper. The sidewalks were crowded.

"We'd better get off Main Street," said Brother
Petrey as he took my arm and steered me up a pre-
cipitous side street. "It would take us until noon to
walk that other block in the center of town."

I could well believe that. From the richest to the
poorest; from the most ignorant to the best educated;
from the successful businessman to the grimy coalpit
worker; from the gracious lady to the black hotel por-
ter—it seemed that everyone knew Brother Petrey and
wanted to take time out to talk with him.

We climbed the steep sidewalk toward Brother
Petrey's home. It was about a half mile. Before long
I was puffing slightly. I glanced at my companion. He
strolled up the inclined walk with an effortless swing.
He carried his eighty-two years lightly.

My last observation is for Christians only: *We'll never
grow old if we keep on working for our Lord.*

All Christians become distressed when the infirmities of
age restrict their religious activities. They begin to feel
useless; sometimes, even guilty—as though they, themselves,
were somehow responsible for the irreversible march of
time. Most important, they no longer feel needed in the service to which they have devoted the greater part of their
lives. Certain church responsibilities require more nervous
and physical energy than they can muster so they have
to give up positions of leadership. They cannot even attend
the worship and other services as they once could. Their

problem is real, disquieting.

Perhaps it is time we redefined what we mean by "working for the Lord." The old saying, "More things are wrought by prayer than this world dreams of," would help us here. That word "wrought" is simply the past tense and the past participle of "work." Then we work when we pray. How weak do we have to become physically before we are unable to pray? From my own experience, I would rather have one blessed old saint praying for me than to have a whole army kicking up the dust!

Most of us, no matter what our physical weakness tells us, can do more than pray.

Mrs. H. W. Witt was a little, white-haired great-grandmother in our church. She had been confined to her bed for many months. One day a young man from the state department of public welfare came to see her. He had some official papers in his hand. Mrs. Witt was going to require lengthy hospitalization and because of her age and financial condition, was being given some monetary assistance.

The young man asked for the deed to the little house in which Mrs. Witt lived. He wanted to examine it. She motioned to a steel document box on the dresser and the young man brought the box to her. She extracted a copy of the deed. While he looked it over, the young man said, "Do you have any other property?"

The tiny pain-wracked Christian woman said, brightly, "Oh, yes; I have. I have a deed to a place that is really a mansion."

Startled, the young man said, "Where is the deed to that?"

"Here in my Bible. I'll show you." She opened the Book.

The young man reached over, expecting to receive a piece of paper, but there was none.

"Where is the deed?" he asked.

Then, Mrs. Witt read to the young man from the welfare office the entire fourteenth chapter of John. Then she said, "If you want it, you can have a deed to the same kind of mansion."

As long as we can talk, or write, we can serve the Lord; we can be working in his vineyard. This will not keep us young in years, but it will keep us young in heart. What is more, we'll receive the highest kind of pay.

Previous mention was made of Brother A. S. Petrey, the mountain preacher. I must add this footnote:

One afternoon as we sat on the porch of his vine-covered cottage in Hazard, Kentucky, I asked the great old missionary this question: "What is the greatest single thing that has happened to you during your long ministry in the Cumberlands?"

The grand old preacher did not hesitate. Pointing to a white church building on a hill, he said, "Two Sundays ago I was guest of honor at services held in that church. As we entered the building the ushers gave each person a red rose. I was conducted up to the platform and given a seat by the side of the pastor.

"When the services were almost over, the pastor asked me to stand. Then he said to members of the congregation: 'If Brother Petrey was the one responsible for your finding Christ as your Savior, come up and pin a rose on him.'

They started coming from every part of the room. They pinned roses all over my coat, down my pants legs, all over my back—I felt like a blooming idiot. But I would not trade

those roses for all the hardwood in those hills," and he
swung his arm in a wide arc toward the surrounding mountains, "nor all the coal beneath the surface of the land
and all the gold in Fort Knox!"

The old saint has long since journeyed to that land where
the roses bloom forever. In my mind's eye I can see him
walking through the gates, and I can see them coming from
every direction in heaven, these whom he has won for his
Lord, and I can hear them saying to him: "Thank you,
Brother Petrey; without you, I might never have found the
Way."

The question is: What does it matter if we do grow a
little older, and we work a little longer when we know that
our path ever leads us to that "land where we'll never grow
old"?

"Give Me That Mountain"

Take a look backward in time—some thirty-four centuries.

Do you see that old codger standing over there? His name is Caleb. That means "dog." And is he well-named! Not a Mexican hairless pup that is neither dog nor cat; not a be-ribboned poodle strutting out stiff-legged from Pamela's Pampered Poodle Parlor. No, siree. He's a bulldog. He's an old bulldog.

There he stands, his long beard flicked by the wind and his eyes on the distant heights. He stands straight and tall, and, as he stands, he stretches up a mighty arm and waves it before the people.

"I'm eighty-five years old today, and I am just as much man as I ever was. See that mountain over there? Forty years ago Moses gave that mountain to me. Of course it was full of giants who made us look like grasshoppers. And that is exactly what we acted like—grasshoppers. We hopped right out of there. All the time I was yelling my head off. I said that we could take it then. But no. We've hopped around for forty years. Now, Joshua, you stood with me then. You and I side by side full of faith in God and in our good right arms. We could have turned those slab-sided, muscle-bound, big, bad men into grasshoppers themselves, but, no. We had to listen to the cowards making noises like yowling jackals in the night. All right. The rest of the tribes have their land where they don't have to fight for every inch of it against soldiers so big they look like trees and so mean that they are like lions tearing up little lambs. They have their tame little territories where the wild grass grows and the milk and honey flow. Now I'll take what's mine. Give me that rocky mountain where the sons of Anak strut and bellow. Let me at them! *Give me that mountain and get out of my way!*"

What a man! What an unspeakably wonderful man. That strong right arm of his was all the Social Security he needed. If the Israelites thought that they would give him a farewell dinner and a gold watch and the office girls would kiss him on his bald spot and put the old dog out where the ground was flat and the livin' was easy, they had another think coming. It may be true—I don't know—that you can't teach an old dog new tricks, but this old dog taught his contemporaries a few; and he can teach us some after thirty-four hundred years have spilled their dust over his tracks.

He can teach us that a man is old when he gives up. He is old when he throws in the towel in the battle of life. The saintly Arthur Flake in his delightful little book *Life at Eighty—As I See It* objected to being called "an old dog" but he sounded a lot like Caleb when he wrote:

"Personally, I have never felt as I imagine most old people feel, judging from the way they appear and act. And yet a young preacher, a friend of mine, thirty-five years ago adjudged me to be an old man. I had just been elected as a field worker by the Baptist Sunday School Board; I was then in my forty-seventh year. This friend was asked what he thought of my fitness for the place and my chances for success. He replied: 'You know that Brother Flake is a salesman and a merchant. I believe he knows Sunday School work, but he could not make a speech to save his life; and you know that you cannot teach an old dog new tricks.' This was my reply: 'My friend is wrong on at least three counts: first, making good speeches and building good Sunday Schools are not the same thing by a long shot; second, I am not old; and third, I am not a dog! Excepting these three little mistakes, his remarks are eminently correct.'"

Had you tried to argue with Arthur Flake even in his eightieth year about the value of Sunday School records, especially the six-point record system which he devised, or had you challenged him upon the necessity of regular visitation of absentees and prospects, or even upon the usefulness of the organized Sunday School class, you would have heard from him a deep-throated growl, not at all dissimilar from that of a bulldog.

Arthur Flake finally moved on into heaven, but while he was on the earth he *lived* every inch of the way. He never felt old, and he never got old.

At the age of twenty-two I became pastor of a small

half-time church in Hagerman, New Mexico. As mentioned previously, I also served as editor of *The Hagerman Messenger,* a weekly newspaper. The latter job was nothing but fun. Without it, I could not have survived as pastor where my salary was thirty-five dollars monthly—when I got it.

Shortly after moving on the field I was out getting acquainted with my members. A few miles out of town I came to the productive farm of Deacon A. M. Ehret—then past eighty. After a short visit with Mrs. Ehret, I was told that I could find her husband out back. Accordingly, I made my way out into the backyard and called his name. I got an answer. It seemed to come down from heaven. Brother Ehret was on the top of a sixty-foot-high windmill tower, which supported a ten-foot wheel. I yelled up my introduction to him, and he called back down: "Glad to see you. Come on up."

Now I am not acrophobic to the point of its being a mental disease, but I was not about to ascend that windmill tower and hold a casual conversation sixty feet up in the air. "Deacon," I called, "if you are going to talk with me, it will be down here on *terra firma.*"

In running through some of my old newspaper files one day, I read that A. M. Ehret had won an automobile race back in 1909. He drove his brass-trimmed racer down a neighboring road at forty miles an hour. That was something else in those days.

One day Olsen's Terrible Swedes came to town. These giants were about seven feet tall and had flaming red beards. They would have stood out in any crowd. In case you don't remember, this was a "Gee-Whiz" basketball team.

They acted like the Harlem Globetrotters, except they
were a different color. The Swedes were in town to play
our town basketball team, New Mexico champions, in an
exhibition game.

Now in that little town of eight hundred souls, basketball was the number one sport. Nothing else happened
when a big game was on. You didn't even dare to die.
This big contest was on Wednesday evening at prayer meeting time. I dutifully went down to the church building.
Deacon Ehret was sitting in his car. He rolled the window
down. "C'mere," he commanded. I went.

Then the old (pardon, superannuated) deacon said,
"Nobody else is coming to prayer meeting. The first quarter
will start in a few minutes. I propose that I'll pray for you
and you'll pray for me and then we'll go see the Swedes. I
already have two tickets."

We joined the rest of the church at the high school gym
and prayed a little and yelled a lot for our town team which,
if I remember correctly, trailed by exactly ninety-six points
at the end of the game. My deacon sat right still for a long
moment after the game was over. I heard him say: "Forgive
the parson and me, Lord. Next time we'll stay at church."

When I preached Deacon Ehret's funeral we had to hold
the services in the front yard at the farm because no building
in town could hold the crowd. People came from up and
down the Pecos from Roswell to Carlsbad.

During my eulogy of my dear friend I half expected to see
him rise up in his casket and yell, "Cut out this foolishness,
and let's get back to work!"

Caleb would say, "Amen; let's get to work." That is another lesson the mighty old warrior could teach us. When

I think of him, I am reminded of Brother M. C. Moore, pioneer preacher of New Mexico. Brother Moore was pastor in Lordsburg at the time I was pastor of First Baptist Church in Las Cruces, some one hundred-twenty miles away. By this time I was in my thirties. I was the pastor of a church several times larger than its counterpart in Lordsburg. Las Cruces was called a city and that made me a "city preacher." As such, because of my good clothes, my youth, and maybe—just maybe—a touch of arrogance, I was looked upon with something less than favor by the grizzled cowmen in the Lordsburg congregation. To put the matter bluntly, they were used to one whom they considered to be a real man in their pulpit. Consequently, when I appeared on the scene to preach in a revival meeting, the ranchers barely tolerated me. The going was pretty rough.

This all happened so long ago that some details are hazy in my mind. This was before World War II, and I cannot remember, for instance, the looks of the house in which Brother Moore lived. I recall only that on the back of the cookstove was a blackened granite-ware coffeepot from which the grounds were never dumped until they almost reached the spout. The brew in that pot looked like the green scum on some stagnant swamp pool. It was delicious.

We were relaxing this particular Saturday afternoon before what we were sure would be a most strenuous Sunday. Brother Moore poured us a couple of cups of his piping hot cowboy coffee that, I am sure, would have floated a horseshoe, if it had not eaten it up.

"You know," he said, "I've got to resign as pastor. I turned seventy last week, and there seems to be an unwritten law that a fellow is all washed up at sixty-five.

I have stretched the limits of that law by about five years."
He paused with my cup half-filled and fixed me with his
deep-set eyes. I began to feel uncomfortable under his
steady gaze. The old fellow finished filling my cup and
continued his complaint. "Here I am, just seventy. I
can still jump a five-rail fence, but they say that I am too
old to preach." He set the coffeepot down on the stove
and stomped over to a high cupboard. He reached up and
took a heavy revolver down. He brought it over and thrust
it into my hands. "See this old 'thumb-buster' single
action? I can still knock down a running jack with it at
fifty yards—

"But, Brother Moore," I interrupted, "what good is that
in your pastoral work? The last time I noticed it was against
the law to shoot deacons."

"God's law or man's?" the old fellow chortled as he took
the heavy Colt .45 revolver from my hands. "I mean that
here am I, an *hombre* that can jump a five-rail fence, with
eyes good enough to shoot the head off a running jackrabbit,
and that means that I've got good muscular coordination
and good nerves and good self-control and all that; but I
am too old to stand up and preach or to drive out to some
ranch and visit the sick. It just ain't right!"

And it really wasn't.

Amos Alonzo Stagg, after a distinguished career as head
coach of the University of Chicago, committed the crime
of becoming seventy years old. That was in 1933. He left
Chicago and took a coaching position at the little College
of the Pacific, just sixty miles from my home now. At the
age of eighty he was elected "Coach of the Year." I met
this grand old man when he was ninety-two. I can still feel

the steel-like grip as he almost crushed my hand. Amos Alonzo Stagg retired of his own accord in 1961. He was then ninety-eight years young, as he put it, but he thought that he should give some other man the chance to coach what was then the University of the Pacific's outstanding football team. When Stagg was one hundred, they gave him a birthday party to celebrate his full century of active years. He made a little speech in which he said, with a twinkle in his voice, "I may go on forever because statistics show that few men died after the age of one hundred." In March, 1965, Amos Alonzo Stagg made his last touchdown. He died in his sleep.

Take another look at that old bulldog, Caleb. See the fire in his eyes, the steel in his arm, and feel the unconquered determination of his spirit. Hear again the homespun proof of Preacher Moore that he was still man enough to get the job done. Listen to the immortal gridiron general, Amos Alonzo Stagg, cracking jokes with a voice which even one hundred years could not make shaky, and who, at ninety, was still winning games.

Each of them was saying to life: Throw a mountain across my way and I will walk right over it. He was saying: Put me on a shelf and I will kick it into splinters.

There are two ways to die. In one of them, they lower one into the grave after due and proper ceremony. They may even toss in a few flowers to close the deal. In the other way to die, one lowers himself and buries himself *alive.*

Would you make your last years your happiest? Then remember this: happiness is a by-product. It cannot be assaulted and won. It cannot be given to you by someone—

anyone else. It cannot be bought with Social Security
benefits, no matter how much increased. Happiness is the
by-product of usefulness. It comes from our being busy
about the right things: values which will outlast ourselves.

Many have found and have traveled this royal road to
happiness in the latest years of their lives. With their
hours no longer ruled by the tyranny of timetables and
calendars, and activities prescribed by set patterns of em-
ployment, they have been free to choose, to innovate, to
be what they have always wanted to be. They have become
able to practice the finest of the fine arts: living life at
its best.

Some, of course, have merely extended their well-formed
habits and occupations with no regard for years. Plato,
at eighty, was still at work, his golden tongue unmuted and
his tremendous mind unclouded. Michelangelo was going
strong at ninety, his sculpturing chisels and mallets flying as
they did in his youth, but flying even more certainly. Titian
at ninety-four was painting what many acclaim to be his
masterpiece. Grandma Moses, of our own times, who
painted her first picture at seventy-six, then one thousand
paintings later, when she was one hundred, was still agile
with sunset-tinted brush. Noah Webster, old as was Caleb,
began the compilation of a new dictionary . . . .

The list could cover every page of this chapter. There is
one trouble about it, though, insofar as I am concerned.
I am tempted to say, "So, what? These are famous, talented
people: philosophers, painters, sculptors, literary per-
sonages of great achievement who never had to retire because some policy said so."

Consequently, since this is a very personal book, I have decided to give, throughout, examples from the lives of persons whom I know or have known intimately. This is not to say that these are "ordinary" people in the usual sense of the word, but it is to affirm that they are people like us—from the average walks of life. What does it matter to me if Grandma Moses could paint beautiful pictures when she was one hundred if I could not even draw the picture of an egg when I was eighteen?

Therefore, let me introduce you to one of the dearest friends my wife and I ever made. Mabel King Beeker, of Nashville, Tennessee, was associate editor of *The Baptist Training Union Magazine* and its successor, *Church Training,* twenty-six years. She has never married. Mabel lived with her mother in a cosy upstairs apartment until her mother's death, then stayed on in the same place surrounded by family heirlooms and mementos of trips in faraway countries which she had visited.

My friendship with Mabel grew out of my own contribution of an inspirational feature to every issue of the magazine over a period of twelve years. Several times I just got tired of writing the stories and wanted to quit. Then a little note would come from Mabel urging me to continue and paying me the highest compliment of all: "They help me."

When the time came for Mabel to retire, I was far more worried about it than was she. "The Magazine," as she called it, had been her life. Attractive as she is, Mabel had never taken a husband. She was married to her work, in which she was outstanding. Her co-workers in the Church Training Department, housed in the huge Baptist Sunday

School Board complex, coined a new word. They said that
once a manuscript had been "Mabelized," there was no question about its being ready for publication. How could Mabel
bear retirement? This is the question that I asked myself in
my anxiety. On a recent trip to Nashville I found out. (It
would take a book this long to tell it.)

Mabel King Beeker's "retirement" includes some part-time
editorial work. She has been able to give herself almost full-
time to her work with internationals, both students and
families. She, who has no family of her own, now has families from all over the world. Her work with international
families has earned for Mabel the distinction of being a
grandmother without having any children. She proudly
displays pictures of Oriental children as she explains how
she became "grandmother" to each of them. In one case,
a Japanese child's mother could not attend church because
of illness. Mabel volunteered to take the three-year-old to
Sunday School each week. Soon the child gave her the title
"Sunday School Grandmother." One Chinese father was
so grateful to the petite gray-haired lady that he asked his
two children if they would like for Miss Beeker to be their
American grandmother. "Oh, yes!" they both exclaimed.
Later a third child born into that family was named
Christina Mabel—thus linking the names Christ and Mabel.

Mabel teaches English to the internationals ("so that we
can communicate"), takes them on trips, and looks after
their spiritual welfare. These are only a small part of the
activities of this dedicated little woman who laughed at
retirement and turned it into the most satisfying part of
her life. Her sublime faith dissolved the mountains of fear
and frustration as water melts sugar. Instead of time weigh-

ing heavily on her hands, she is unable to find enough of it to do what love commands.

Please meet another little woman who was married to her work and for whom retirement was almost like divorce. My wife's aunt, Ruth Hatch, managed a large abstract and title company in Albuquerque, New Mexico, for many years. Although she would have made a wonderful wife for any man, she never had a husband. Instead, she gave herself to caring for her mother and shared her home with two crippled brothers until the deaths of all three. Ruth was devoted to her work. Hours meant nothing to her; they were long and hard, but filled with the sense of accomplishment.

Ruth made a good salary in her responsible position, and she invested her earnings so successfully that she probably has all the money she needs for the rest of her life. She has always been quick to respond to the financial needs of other members of her family. Ruth is the only relative I have ever had (and she is in my wife's name) who managed to get together enough dollars to count.

I have always loved the independent little whipper-snapper. I wondered what the effect of retirement would be on cheerful little Ruth whose whole life was in her work. I need not have worried. She reeled with the blow but soon recovered. She still lives in the big house fronting on Rio Grande Park and looks after it, her lawn, and flowers as best she can. But this is not all. One day every week, regular as clockwork, she shows up at the Red Cross center and works. Another day is given to work at the blood bank. Other charitable occupations take up any slack in her time. She, too, has found the secret of happiness—being busy at something worthwhile.

There is a man whom I do not know, but I would dearly like to. I am certain that I will not meet him this side of heaven. I have only heard his voice. He is now ten years older than was Caleb when he demanded, as his share of the Promised Land, the only part not conquered: the mountain filled with giants. This man, nearing the century mark, is still tackling his own kind of mountain, totally unafraid.

My young friend, Ross West of Franklinton, Louisiana, with whom I was discussing this proposed book, mailed to me a recorded speech by this most remarkable man.

In a clear, firm voice, the talk begins: "I am Charles S. Chapman, Louisville, Kentucky. I have been invited to speak at the Kenwood Baptist Church on Layman's Sunday, January 26. May I share with you the outline of my proposed speech?"

Then, in his own words, uttered with simplicity, humility, and dignity, this grand old man unfolds a short sketch of his life. The talk revolves around the two most important decisions he ever made. His two great commitments came when he was sixteen years of age.

He describes the custom of his boyhood days for a lad to wear knee-length pants with long, black, cotton stockings until he was sixteen at which time he could graduate to full-length trousers and be classified as a "young man." He had been going to Sunday School regularly, but not to church. His older sister, Bertha, told him that if he would go to the church services with her, she would buy him his first long trousers. "They cost two dollars," he says, "but they were a wonderful investment." He started going to the worship services, and, he says, "From that day on the church has enriched my life."

Chapman describes how he trusted Christ and was invited to the deacons' meeting on Friday night for examination to see whether or not he was qualified to join the church. He was approved by deacons and church and was baptized. Then in a quiet voice, tremulous with emotion, the nonagenarian explains, "From that time on God and I have been developing a closer walk together. Here am I, ninety-three. Next month I will be ninety-four. I know that we have a great God. He holds our destiny. We can trust him."

"Now," the speaker says, "what about that second most important decision?" The rhetorical question is answered by the description of how, as the ushers in the church walked down the aisle to receive the offering, the pastor quoted these words from the Bible: "Bring ye all the tithes into the storehouse, that there may be meat in mine house, and prove me now herewith, saith the Lord of hosts, if I will not open you the windows of heaven, and pour you out a blessing, that there shall not be room to receive it" (Mal. 3:10).

The young man decided to tithe, and he kept it up the rest of his life. His first job was in a men's clothing store on Saturday afternoons and evenings. At the end of the first Saturday, he went to the cashier's cage and was handed a half dollar. He turned it over in his hands and said, "I can't tithe that." He went back to the cashier and asked for change, receiving a quarter, two dimes and a nickel. He put the nickel in his left pants pocket and said, "That belongs to God." He put the rest in his right pants pocket and said, "That belongs to me." Chapman says that from that day in 1897 to the present hour he has not missed giving his tithe.

The chronicle of Chapman's life continues with his experiences from job to job, tells about his marriage in 1908, his children whom he saw through college, and always, no matter what happened to him, God kept his word and poured out his blessings. He was never without sufficient money for his needs and those of his family. Probably the most interesting of all the episodes was Chapman's association with James L. Kraft of the far-flung Kraft Enterprises. Kraft did a favor for me personally in the early days of my writing. He bought twelve copies of my first book. My own admiration of this great Christian gentleman knew no bounds. So my ears pricked up as Chapman developed his speech. He had taken a job with Stewart Warner in Chicago, "because they had two problems that they could not solve." He says that "God and I licked those two problems," but he had worked himself right out of a job. He and his wife had united with North Shore Baptist Church, where Kraft was chairman of deacons. Kraft was having problems with an emulsifying process for salad dressing, and he invited Chapman to help solve that. The speaker tells how he developed a special piece of machinery by making a wooden model first, then adding more horsepower. From this effort came "Miracle Whip Salad Dressing." Then, he says, with a chuckle, "That is my baby."

But, again, Chapman had worked himself right out of a job. He developed a 16 mm sound movie projector to be used for educational purposes for another firm. This took nine months, and he was looking for work again. He moved to Louisville and worked fourteen years with a big engineering concern, but had to give it up when he was seventy-four. Another engineering firm wanted him, and he says, with pardonable pride, "I received two 10 percent raises in my late seventies." This concern retired Chapman at the age of eighty, but he was soon employed again. His last engineering position was taken at the age of eighty-seven! Each time Chapman describes his jobs, he says with a ring to his voice, "And I enjoyed my work."

The speech ends with these words: "I would like to tell you about three sentences that I read about twenty-five years ago. Nothing that I had read previously had grabbed my mind the way these three sentences did. They were written by Dr. George W. Truett, of Dallas, Texas. 'To know God is the greatest discovery. To know God's will is the greatest wisdom. To do God's will is the greatest accomplishment.' "

* * *

What a ringing challenge! Do you not feel like tackling your own mountain, now? I do.

Dr. J. B. Tidwell, the renowned Bible scholar, was about sixteen when he wrote on the flyleaf of his arithmetic book: "J. B. Tidwell + God = Enough." It is so.

5

"My Heart Is Fixed"

One month before I retired, my little mother-in-law, wearing her ninety years as lightly as a crocheted shawl, flew up from San Diego to visit us.

I chided her for getting up so early in the morning. At five o'clock, she was already up, puttering around in the kitchen, fixing coffee for herself, going out into the backyard—doing everything but what I thought she ought to be doing—sleeping until a decent hour.

"Why don't you stay in bed a little longer—at least until daybreak?" I demanded, as I sleepily groped my way into the darkened living room.

"And miss the sunrise?" she asked. "I wouldn't do God that way—"

"You wouldn't do God what way?"

"Refuse to receive his gift of the sunrise."

I opened my mouth—then closed it very slowly, my

flippant reply dead on my lips. I had started to say, "God will keep on making the sun to rise whether you watch it or not," or—"God has made the sun to come up millions of times, and he certainly wouldn't care if you failed to see one of them," or—"Just because he makes the sun come up, he doesn't expect you to jump out of bed to watch it."

"I don't like the dark," said my little mother-in-law, "I don't like the long nights. You know, the nights get pretty long when your old body aches all over so you can hardly sleep at all. Then finally the sun comes up. The birds begin to sing. Listen."

From the many trees in my backyard came the birdsong. I walked to the patio door and looked upward. On the very top of the seventy-five foot high redwood which I planted twenty years ago, a mockingbird swang to and fro and a steady trill of notes sifted down through the needles to lie momentarily on the feathery ferns below. Another mockingbird on a swaying limb of the big plum tree joined in a duet and even as I stood there, that cloudless morning, the birds sang the sun up into the sky.

My mother-in-law made her way out into the fresh morning, breathing deeply. She turned back to me, her face radiant as that of an angel. "The birds make me think of David. In one of the psalms he says that he is going to wake up the morning with his song. He had had a hard night, too, but the only ache that he had—the worst of all—was in his heart."

"Now, wait a cotton-pickin' minute," I said, irreverently, "I don't remember reading anything like that in the Bible—"

"It's there. I read it just yesterday. It's right in the fifty-seventh Psalm. I read some of the psalms every day. You

see, with these cataracts and everything else that's wrong
with my eyes, I may not be able to read much longer.
That is also why I like to see the sunrise and the sunset
and look up at the stars and see the beauty of the
flowers. . . ."

I was glad that she could not see my sudden tears. I
turned back into the living room. In a few minutes she
came over to where I had settled down with the morning
paper, which I had retrieved from the damp grass of the
front yard. My coffee cup, its contents steaming hot, was
in my hand. I was sipping coffee and gobbling up the
headlines.

"Here," she said, "put that trash down and read something worthwhile."

Now, I have held this little woman in awe for at least
fifty years. She took her place in my heart then, about
the time my own mother died, and she has been my
mother—the only one I have had—these many years. My
awe of her began when she walked into her front room
that night so long ago and found me with her daughter
sitting on my lap.

"Ina," she said, frigidly, "is that the only chair in the
room?"

My blushing wife-to-be landed half across the room
in one jump. Through the forty-nine years of our marriage I have been afraid to let Ina sit on my lap for fear
her mother might come into the room. Well, anyway, I
have held the little mother-in-law in the deepest respect,
not unmingled with a touch of fear. When she laid the
book of Psalms with its big print on top of my morning
paper, I obediently began to read it. Soon I laid my paper

aside and went into my study.

Question: How did my saintly little mother-in-law know my deepest need, no matter how I tried to cover it up? How could she have sensed the unnamed fear which ate at my vitals when I would not even admit it to myself?

Deep in my heart I know the answer. This valiant little soul herself has bent like a willow in the winter gales, but she has been broken by no storm. She has followed a hearse twelve times and has stood by open graves which have received the mortal remains of closest loved ones: father, mother, six brothers and sisters, one baby son, two married daughters, and, the hardest of all to bear, the body of her beloved husband.

The husband, my wife's father, Gordon Hollaway, was killed in an accident connected with a quick-silver mining venture during World War II. He was thrown from a pickup truck on a rough road in the Big Bend country of Texas. The mine, with its mineral needed for the war effort, was right on the Mexican border. Ina's older sister Lila, her brother David, and I, went to the mine headquarters to try to settle insurance matters and it was, without doubt, the wildest country I had ever seen. The men wore big revolvers as they did one hundred years ago. Fierce-looking Yaqui Indians roamed the hills, worked in the mine, and fished in the Rio Grande. My father-in-law, a Baptist deacon, had been in town—Alpine—to get materials for a Sunday School class for the Indians, who loved him greatly. Lying by his body, when it was found, were quarterlies and other Sunday School materials which had been thrown from the cab of the truck.

The death of her husband left my little mother-in-law to

face what has been by now about thirty-five years of lone-
liness. If she ever complained, I never knew it.

The last time that she stood by an open grave, it was at
the funeral of a beloved son-in-law—the thirteenth loved
one she has had to mourn. She has known what it means
to be hungry, physically, as well as in the heart. Pain and
suffering have left some lines in her face but laughter comes
quick to her, and it sounds like the tinkling of a bell. Even
now, at ninety, she is looking after a granddaughter and
her little daughter because they are in need.

That is how I know how *she* knows, and cares, about
my own troubled heart.

I stayed in my study two hours with my mother-in-law's
well-worn copy of the book of Psalms open before me. Of
course I had read the words many times before. I *needed*
to read them now. That made the difference.

                              * * *

David was hiding in the cave of Adullam. He was fleeing
from Saul, who sought his life. As he ventured to the mouth
of the grotto, he could see Saul's army camped on the opposite hillside. Not only were there enemies in front of
him but he knew, all too painfully, that some among his
own soldiers were spies who would betray him at their
first opportunity. Besides the human enemies almost surrounding his hiding place, there were wild animals in the
wilderness ready to rend him with claw and fang. Most
of all there was a fearful enemy in his own heart. It
forced him, now, to find shelter in the shadows as he looked
out. Were he to expose himself for one moment in the
light of the sun an arrow would find its deadly mark. A cry
of anguish rose softly to the lips of the fugitive.

As my eyes followed the words of the psalm that morning I realized, what my mother-in-law had sensed, that I had taken refuge in my own little psychological cave. Before me was no army equipped with spears, swords, or bows and arrows, nor even with nuclear warheads. My foes were impalpable, but just as deadly. The hills before my own cosy little cave were the figurative rough country of retirement, what my Mexican friends call *mal pais*—badlands. Within this wilderness strode the giants of boredom, uselessness, financial insecurity, ill-health, and dozens of unnamed others. This was an army shooting from the drawn bows of circumstance, arrows dipped in slow-acting poison.

I turned the pages backward to Psalm 55. This threnody of anguish relates to a problem which I have never known: the rejection of a father by a child. We have four grown children, with families, now, of their own. Not once did one of them ever bring us a single hour of pain or doubt about their integrity. Not so, poor David. Not only was he rejected by Absalom, but in the heart of that son was hate and murder. In his despair the psalmist cried out:

"O that I had wings like a dove!
for then would I fly away and be at rest."

But, where could David fly? Where, indeed, can a man fly away from himself? Deep inside him, he knew better than that for he cried in another place: "If I take the wings of the morning, and dwell in the uttermost parts of the sea; even there shall thy hand lead me and thy right hand shall hold me" (Ps. 139:9-10).

The troubled man could neither fly away from his own heart on the wings of time, nor, what is more important,

could he fly away from God. He must find his peace
where he was or he could not find it at all.

Moving on to Psalm 56, right in the middle of it, I
found the answer to my own disquiet even as David did
his, thirty centuries ago. He frankly faced up to his
fear. He neither denied it to himself nor did he try to
cover it from his consciousness. Neither, we can thank-
fully say, did he try to cover it up from us, or there would
be no lesson here. Except from his own revelation, which
of us would ever suspect that this most stalwart of men
ever faced the winds of panic blowing through his own
soul? Fixed in our memory is the picture of a stripling
youth whose only weapon was a slingshot with a pouch
of five smooth stones walking resolutely toward a giant in
blazing armor nine feet tall; or of the same lad grown to
manhood whose ears rang with the song of the women:
"Saul hath slain his thousands, and David his ten thousands." How could such a superman know any fear at
all? Yet, here are his words: "My heart is sore pained
within me: and the terrors of death are fallen upon me,
and horror hath overwhelmed me." Then in the middle
of Psalm 56, the indomitable warrior cried, "What time
I am afraid I will trust in thee." He took his tears one by
one and dropped them like glistening pearls into a bottle
held in the hand of God.

I caught my breath for a long moment, thinking. Then
I read on. In Psalm 57 David has at last found his wings.
They are not the fragile wings of a dove, but the mighty
wings of the Master of all storms: they are the very wings
of God. Then ringing from the heart of David, and bounc-
ing down the slopes of the mountain, comes the shout of

the man who is no longer afraid, "Yea, in the shadow of thy wings will I make my refuge."

Listen to it, Saul. Listen well, you would-be-murderer! You are hearing the shout of a man with whom *God* fights. In these ringing words you are hearing your doom!

Suddenly the sweet singer of Israel has found his song again, and what a song it is! He will wake up the morning with its joyous melody ("I will stir up the morning dawn").

This is the song *"My heart is fixed, O God, my heart is fixed."*

I closed the book of the Psalms and bowed my own head in prayer. God heard my cry and put a new song in my heart. Instead of the notes of fear that had dinned in raucous discordance, there came the sweet notes of faith and hope. Let me share my song with you.

It is a song of hope in a land of fear because *my heart is fixed on God, my heavenly Father.*

My wife and I drove across Golden Gate Bridge late in the afternoon. The sun, like a huge, orange basketball, sank without a splash into the sparkling water, setting the famed Golden Gate aflame with wavering sheets of crimson glory.

The mighty arches of the bridge reached from the burning water below up to the multilaned highway in the sky, then changed form to become two mighty towers climbing up, up, into the gathering dusk. From each tower gracefully swung the three-foot thick encapsulated cables which, like great rust-colored pipes, swooped downward again in smooth curves. In San Francisco the bridge began; in the green-clad hills of Marin County it landed, and the highway flowed into a tiled tunnel with its mixture of fog and fluorescent lights ever aglow.

The reverent soul could not help but marvel at the awe-inspiring works of God and man in such juxtaposition. God's work: the faintly-colored sky with a lone white cloud drifting lazily by; the dancing colors on the heaving breast of the ocean named "Peaceful"; the wide sweep of the velvety green of the smooth hillsides; gulls floating effortlessly on the whispering breeze . . . all this fired the wondering imagination and compelled worship. Man's work: an engineering marvel of concrete and steel spanning a mile of deep water, the gateway to the world; a purposeful steamer threading its way along the channel, Orient-bound, and behind it three lazy fishing craft rocking toward Fisherman's Wharf and the Embarcadero and all around, as far as the eye could see, tiny white sails like the fluttering wings of moths, dotting the golden waters. Shakespeare could have cried anew, "What a piece of work is man!"

"What beauty!" murmured my wife in rapture, her face like that of a little girl looking wonderingly into a kaleidoscope.

"Yes," I said, softly, with a wonder of my own, "God and man working together can build like this."

The next morning a San Francisco newspaper described how, that very night, an automobile suddenly veered from the outer lane of Marin-bound traffic, up to the sidewalk. A well-dressed, gray-haired man leaped from the car, leaving the motor running. He scrambled up the low parapet toward the void, stood for a breathless moment, then leaped up and outward.

An antisuicide patrol car screeched to a halt but too late. Soon its mobile phone was reporting, somewhat wearily, that another human body lay broken on the water two hundred-forty-six feet below. At the time of this writing, five hundred thirty-six people have jumped from this bridge, all but eight of them into eternity. This, from the outer barricades of "The Most Beautiful Bridge in the World." Officers of the law in patrol cars cruise the lanes of the bridge every minute of the day and night with only one duty to perform: to protect a living soul from himself.

I read where one of the last of these who succumbed to the suicide syndrome of the Bridge was a successful business man. What caused his desperate act of self-destruction? Listen to his widow: "He was despondent. He had reached the age of sixty-five and was forced to give up his work by retirement. His work was his life. Faced with the prospects of giving up what, to him, was all that gave any significance to life, he simply couldn't take it. He said to me not long ago, 'If I have to be a nobody, then I'll stop being anybody at all.' I have lived in constant fear of this."

Of course the motivations of the bridge suicides run the whole gamut of human emotions, but the question is: How many others, faced with what they imagined to be their "phasing out of life," decided to go all the way in one wild moment?

One thing seems certain. Every one of these who loosed the "silver cord" with his own hands and plunged to death to lie, like the pitcher of Ecclesiastes, broken on the waves below, stumbled over the fatal word: hopelessness.

Hope, like faith, is the gift of God who is our Father. No one else can give it to us. Among the ingredients of this hope is the faith that our heavenly Father will still find work for us to do that we can retain our sense of worth.

Elijah sat under the juniper tree and the hot sun beat

down upon him. Tears of self-pity dropped from his eyes to the sand and rolled into little balls of despair. He wanted to die—but at the hands of the Lord. "O Lord, take away my life."

Have you been there, friend?

Have you been fed by the angel of the Lord?

God still needed Elijah upon the earth. Who else, among men, could bring Ahab to the dust?

God still needs *you.* He still needs me. Listen to the still small voice as hope whispers in the needles of the juniper tree.

* * *

As I read the words of David that morning in my study, I felt a sweet happiness settling over my soul, and my heart, like a drifting sailboat, found its anchor under the shadow of his wings.

My song is a song of peace in a land of strife because *my heart is fixed on Jesus, the "Prince of Peace."*

It was a balmy Sunday afternoon. I was fifteen. I was muffing flies on a sandlot ball diamond in Albuquerque, New Mexico (I was never a very good baseball player).

My high-school buddy, Perris Woodruff, found me at the close of the game and invited me to go to a revival with him down at old First Baptist at Lead and Broadway. I had never been in a Baptist church, but such was the earnest invitation of my friend that I consented. That night, when the invitation was given, Perris put his arm around me. "Don't you want to trust Christ and confess him as your Savior?" In a moment I was in the aisle and moving toward the preacher. My feet were much lighter then than they had been on the baseball diamond. A weight had been lifted from my spirit—and it never came back.

After my baptism, one Wednesday night I gave my testimony. It consisted of a single verse of Scripture, Philippians 4:13: "I can do all things through Christ which strengtheneth me." I believed it all the way to my retirement—then forgot it and had to relearn it.

Then, one Sunday night, Pastor T. F. Harvey preached a sermon on "What is that in thine hand?" from the story of Moses and his rod, which, when he cast it on the ground, became a serpent from which he fled in fear. Brother Harvey was one of the greatest expository preachers I have ever known. He made each of us stand before his own burning bush and listen to God's call. Then he invited all who would surrender their lives for special Christian service to make their way down to the altar. Twenty-two young people responded. Russell Goff, his brother Cecil, Perris Woodruff, and I became successful preachers and pastors. Tom Wiley became a Christian educator, reelected just as often as the state constitution permitted to the position of New Mexico State Superintendent of Public Instruction.

I can't remember all who went forward that night, but I *do* remember that a pretty girl came down the aisle with the others and just happened to stand by my side. I was not going with her then, but, if God lets us live another year, to December 21, 1977, we shall have walked together as husband and wife one hundred years—fifty each. Most of the volunteers that night attended Montezuma Baptist College near Las Vegas, lost to Baptists now, since 1932. Of course the storms of life struck us all, but, so far as I know, everyone of that score and more young people made

good. 'Tis blessed—this peace beyond all understanding!
Only Jesus can give it and only willing hearts can receive
it.

> "When peace, like a river, attendeth my way,
> When sorrows like sea billows roll;
> Whatever my lot, Thou hast taught me to say,
> It is well, it is well with my soul."

My song is a song of power in a land of frustration
because *my heart is fixed on the Holy Spirit as my Guide.*

My father, Harvey, was a fine violinist. He could play
with such power as to make the angels weep with envy.
I do not know whether or not there will be any violins
in heaven, but if so, I want to sit at his feet and hear him
play again.

It seems to me that his sweetest music came after my
mother died, and he was left alone to try to bring up four
children. I could hear him in his bedroom, late at night,
playing softly—for himself alone, or—maybe Mother.

When I was a little boy, in Tulsa, Oklahoma, my father
took me to hear the immortal Fritz Kreisler. He could
not afford seats on the lower floor of the large auditorium,
and we sat in one of the balconies, far away from the
brightly-lighted stage.

Kreisler played his concert. My father leaned forward
as far as he could, to get every tonal quality drifting upward
toward our listening ears. I endured the music as any little
boy would, but I shall never forget the last number—nor
would I wish to do so.

We had thought the presentation finished. Applause
smashed at the eardrums, and the crowd was on its feet
in a standing ovation that lasted minutes. The violinist

raised his hand, and the tumult subsided.

Suddenly the artist brought his violin up over his head and smashed it down on the floor where it shattered like a box of dropped matches. A huge woman next to us screamed and threw her opera glasses over the balcony rail. There was excited jabbering of voices until the violinist waved for silence. He beckoned and from the wings came a page carrying a violin on a velvet cushion. He picked up the instrument and placed it to his chin, lightly drawing the bow across the vibrating strings. By that time the audience of many thousands had been seated and waited breathlessly.

Kreisler spoke, and here are his words as I remember them: "You have thought that I smashed my Stradivarius. I did not. The violin here," and he nudged the pieces with his toe, "I bought in one of your Tulsa stores for ten dollars. I had heard someone say, 'Of course he can make great music; who couldn't—with a $200,000 violin?' Listen well, my friends, the music is not in the violin but in the heart and touch of the master."

Then Fritz Kreisler played his own composition, "The Last Refrain."

My father started me on the violin when I was seven. He put me in the charge of a stern old teacher, Monsieur Le Grande, but I would not practice. I disappointed my earthly father. So, too, many times I have disappointed my heavenly Father, but if I have ever made any music at all, it has been when I became just a ten-dollar fiddle in the hands of the Master.

That afternoon, mentioned earlier, when as a twenty-two-year-old pastor I was getting acquainted with the members of my new church, I met another whom I would like you to know. He was T. J. Nail.

I was walking along the sidewalk when I heard a deep bass voice singing "Rock of Ages." I followed the voice and came to the porch of a little white house set well back from the road. On the porch a white-haired man rocked back and forth and as he rocked he sang. As I stepped up on the porch, the song stopped. I introduced myself and stuck out my hand, but the old fellow did not take it. He was blind. He sensed my attempt to shake his hand and groped for mine. He gave it a warm squeeze. There flashed through my mind words from the book of Job "who giveth songs in the night."

Paul and Silas sang the doors of their jail open—at midnight!

My song is a song of joy in a land where I am just a pilgrim because my heart is *fixed on heaven as my home.*

One evening, several years ago, I was getting ready to go to church where we were having a revival when my phone rang.

"Are you the pastor of *La Iglesia Bautista?*" asked a feminine voice in heavy Latin accent.

"No, I am not. The pastor of the Spanish church is Brother Enoch Ortega—"

"I do not mean the Spanish church. I mean the Baptist church on Park Avenue. Are you heem?"

"I am," I assured her. "What can I do for you?"

"Well, you see, I am the landlady to Mrs. Perez, who belongs to your church. She has just been operated at the county hospital, and she wants to see you. Can you go now?"

I sent my family on in the car and got behind the wheel of my hunting and fishing Jeep station wagon and turned the battered old vehicle toward the hospital. I have always been glad that I did.

In one of the dismal wards on an upper floor, I found Mrs. Perez. Actually, though her operation had been delicate and major, she was doing well and was in no danger. She apologized for her landlady's call and said there was no urgency about my visit, so I talked just a moment and whispered a prayer.

As I stood to leave, she said, "Do you see that old lady in the second bed over from mine? She is eighty-three years of age and is dying of cancer. I think that she belongs to a church, but she keeps asking a funny question. She asks everybody who comes if they know where the Scripture verse about the tabernacle is found, and nobody knows. I don't know the Old Testament very well; so I can't help her. Won't you go over and tell her?"

I glanced at my watch. It was 7:30. The meeting at the church was just starting, and I was a mile away.

"I am sorry," I answered, "but the services are already beginning, and people will wonder where I am. Besides, she doesn't need to know anything about the tabernacle now. It is just a mental quirk of some kind."

But my eyes were drawn toward the old lady on the third bed. Her snow-white hair mingled with the whiteness of the pillow. Her face was gaunt and worn, etched with the lines of pain.

Suddenly I found myself standing by her bed. "Hello, mother," I said, softly.

The faded old eyes opened, and she gazed at me for a

long moment.

"Doctor, I hurt," she said.

"I am not the doctor," I said gently, "I am pastor of Baptist Temple—"

"Oh, thank God, thank God. Maybe you can tell me where to find that Scripture verse about the tabernacle— you know—the one that says, 'If the tabernacle is destroyed—' "

Quick illumination flooded my mind. Of course! Why had not I known it instantly? Quirk of the mind, indeed! It was the poignant longing of the troubled soul.

I took the thin, nervous hand in my own and bent over the bed. In that moment I wondered about the woman. How had she looked when she was young? Had she been beautiful? Certainly she had been strong and virile. Now she lay in the last moments of life, her body broken by the weight of eighty-three winters and the ravages of disease.

I felt in my pocket for my New Testament, but found that in my haste I had left it at home. I would have to do the next best.

"The Scripture verse you want is found in the fifth chapter of Second Corinthians, the first verse. Listen: 'For we know that if our earthly house of this tabernacle were dissolved, we have a building of God, an house not made with hands, eternal in the heavens.' "

"That's it!" cried the aged patient. "I remembered that it had an 'if' in it, and it worried me."

I said it again. "It does have an *if* in it, but that *if* refers to the destruction of this old body; and *if* it is dissolved, then we *know*—no 'if' there—that God will give us a new body and that we will live with him forever in that land beyond all tears and pain and death."

The lines on the tired old face dissolved into a quiet smile; and then the old lady spoke calmly, all fear gone: "Thank you, Brother, for stopping by my bed. I never saw you before and I'll never see you again in this world, but I'll say hello to you in heaven."

The drab old county hospital ward had suddenly become the vestibule to heaven and angels were hovering around a certain bed.

That is why I showed up at church just in time for the sermon. Everybody wondered where I had been, but how could I ever explain that I had stopped by heaven on my way there?

6
Upside-down World

There was a saying among the bright young theologues
of Montezuma Baptist College: "If you have to go to hell,
make sure you go there in a Model T. Then you are certain
of getting back." Admittedly the quality of the humor is
poor, and its theological concept faulty, but the observation was soul-felt more than it was flippant. The Model T
Ford was a set of wheels than which there were no whicher.

My own love affair with the brain child of Henry Ford
began with Nancy. Nancy had the tin you loved to touch.
Of course her curves were a little too angular for modern
taste, but I used to run my hand over them and sigh with
a desire that almost consumed me. My love was of the
"bleeding heart" kind. I was sixteen years old and Nancy
belonged to another. The "another" was a pot-bellied
character named Chambers, who operated a grocery store
on South Edith Street in Albuquerque. I was his "boy

Friday" after school and all day Saturday. My main function was to sweep floors, sack potatoes, keep the shelves stocked neatly, take telephone orders in the absence of His Nibs, and make deliveries with Nancy.

Merchant Chambers lived in a modest house far out in University Heights. My own home was farther out toward the mountains. Every Saturday morning I rode my bicycle from Dartmouth Street (the last residential street then) over to East Central Avenue and down to the street where Nancy—pardon—Mr. Chambers lived. I can see him now in what the kids call "the windmill of my mind." Coincident with my arrival on a cold winter's day when my ears were nearly frost-bitten and my face was blue with cold, Old Man Chambers (as I called him behind his back) burst through the front door of his house with a brass tea-kettle in hand, steam hissing from its spout. Draped from head to foot in a long, black overcoat garnished with a white scarf wound around a thick neck, an ear-flapped cap pulled down over his bald head, he looked like a cross between a Russian Bolshevik and a beardless Santa Claus. Back to the sliding garage door he marched, nodding for me to push it open. There stood Nancy (Nancy's predecessor was a sorrel mare once owned by Chambers back in Missouri, "the best gol-darned mare I ever owned"). I always caught my breath so sharply that it whistled. Black, brass-trimmed beauty!

Now commenced the starting ritual, every movement counting. "Spark lever up!" shouted Mr. Chambers.

I reached through the crackling curtain on Nancy's left and moved the spark lever to the top. The lever was located on the left of the steering column. If you forgot to

retard the spark in this manner, you were likely to wear
your arm in splints for six or seven weeks.

"Spark lever up!" I yelled, as though we were cranking
a Curtiss Swallow.

Now this was always *first*.

Next Mr. Chambers grasped the brass radiator cap with
the fingers of his right hand. The radiator cap had four
little protuberances, or ears, on its rounded top. It always
reminded me of the horns on a Viking's headpiece, except
that I had never seen the picture of a four-horned one. But
still, that's what it reminded me of.

With the radiator cap spun off and safely palmed in the
right hand, Nancy's owner gave her a drink of steaming
water down to the fourth gurgle. Next in a quick play
quarter-backed through mental telepathy, teakettle was
passed to me; I made a noninterference run to the front
door of the house. Said door opened; I passed the pot to
the waiting Mrs. Chambers, called back over my shoulder,
"Hi, Mrs. Chambers," spun right, dashed around my boss
to Nancy's right side to hold the door open (there was only
a dummy door on the driver's side of the '25 model, as
you gray-beards will recall).

In the meantime the grocer had thrust his finger through
the choke ring to the left and below the radiator. I forgot
to mention that he always, on these frosty mornings, wore
big, gauntleted gloves. The left one had to be removed in
order for the groceryman to get his finger through the small
choke ring. The leather glove was placed on the hood of
the engine. Mr. Chambers carefully lined his thumb along-
side the crank handle (if you hooked your thumb *over* the
handle in the natural way, you were some kind of nut. Cor-

rection: you were a nut with a busted arm if the motor kicked back).

Mr. Chambers puffed out his fat cheeks in expectation, gave three cranks (count 'em) and the engine snorted into life. ALWAYS. It shook off the glove (invariably). Mr. Chambers stooped over with a big expulsion of breath, snatched up the glove, pulling it on his hand as he squeezed through the door, settled into the seat (safety belts only held your pants up in those days), adjusted the spark lever down five notches to "advance" and in the same movement (like poetry), released the emergency brake handle (which also kept the car in neutral), pressed hard on the left pedal to actuate the low band, pulled down on the gas lever on the *right* of the steering column and we were on our way. By the time we were out of the driveway, Mr. Chambers had eased the left foot pedal back, and we were in high gear headed for his victual emporium some six miles away.

Now, there are those who think that the 747 is quite the cat's meow. Bah! Their idea is conceived, born, and nurtured in colossal ignorance. There is nothing in this world today, absolutely *nothing* in the field of transportation that could possibly give me the feeling of security and tenderness which I felt in those days when I settled back into the arms of Nancy.

(Just you wait, old girl, until I get you out into those sandhills on the delivery runs this afternoon. Boy, I'll turn you loose.)

One day I would have a Nancy of my very own. The day finally came. I had enrolled in Montezuma Baptist College as a ministerial student. The man highest on the

campus totem pole, as I recall it, was Earl Keating. He
owned a Model T coupe, with real glass windows in it. The
administration building, which also contained some light
housekeeping rooms, was on the top of a high hill over-
looking the Gallinas River Canyon. The huge structure, with
its two round turrets piercing the sky, and its four hundred
rooms, looked like a medieval castle. Earl had a preaching
appointment some one hundred miles away, and he drove
his beloved Model T there and back every Sunday. The
trouble was, Earl could not drive straight up that last hill
to the college building with any dignity. He had to turn
around and back up because the middle transmission band,
controlled by the center pedal, was the reverse and was
never as badly worn as was the low band (used every time
the car started to move forward). Earl got so he could drive
up that hill backwards as fast as he could go frontwards.

Louis Crisler somehow got a nice Model T touring car in
which he transported five of us would-be preachers all the
way to the Pecos country where we spread the gospel. How
I envied Louis! (And it was all very moral. The Bible says
that a man is not to covet his neighbor's donkey or his
wife, but it does not say a thing about a Model T.)

Then I found my own Nancy. Boy, was she a broken-
down specimen. She had a chassis, an engine, four wheels,
and a gas tank. (Remember, gray-beards, how the Model T
was gravity fed?) Well, I sat right on that gas tank. On
my preaching trips I kept a sharp lookout for abandoned
Model T's. One woman allowed me to take a windshield
from a wreck in her backyard, another gave me a little
sporting body and before long, I had my own stripped-
down hot-rod. I could never quite get it out of low gear,

and it tried to run over me every time I cranked it—once ran me into a barbed wire fence and tore my new suit pants. Another time I almost froze to death in it during a high country snowstorm, but what a car she was! My Dodge Polara out in my driveway right now only runs when it feels like it. It is what is called a "luxury" automobile. It takes an expert mechanic to change the spark-plugs along with about twenty-five dollars worth of tools. Phooey! I could take a piece of baling wire, a pair of two-bit pliers, and keep that Model T purring like a contented cat. There is one other thing that you older automobile wranglers will remember. The spark was activated by a series of four little coils under the dashboard. We usually left the covers off so if a contact point stuck while we were driving and one plug missed fire, we could reach under there and by feel, loose the vibrator, half the time getting an electric shock that was guaranteed to eject us from our seats!

* * *

Well, friends, the old world has changed. Some of those changes none of us likes. Not only are our automobiles mass-produced and stamped out by huge presses and machines, but human beings are being mass-produced and stamped out by the machines of a soulless, amoral society. You and I are cogs in a vast technological and socio-logical machine over which we have little or no control. We may protest and cry out against it, but who can hear our agonized cries amidst the clanking and the squeaking of the inexorable machine?

The cries, of course, are not just from the older. They come, frighteningly to us, sometimes, from the young as well. The young man said, "I don't like to be like everyone else," so he let his hair grow long and wove it into a braid all tied with a ribbon. He put a string of beads around his muscular neck and suspended a wild-looking hunk of metal from it. He threw his shoes into the garbage can, usually along with his morals. His friend copied him. Soon all looked alike; they acted alike. None of his peers dared to either look or to be any different. The girls discarded their dresses in favor of the dirtiest, raggedest denim pants that they could find (some were just big patches loosely tied together with thread). They ironed their hair and fixed themselves up so you could not tell a girl from a boy and tried to usher in the biological phenomenon of the unisex. When they put on dresses—well, they didn't. Girls and women wore (still do) dresses to church that had less material than their grandmothers put on to go swimming at some secluded beach.

Then came the so-called "free speech movement" accompanied by acts of anarchy which were tolerated because the whole country was afraid of the kids. The only demand for freedom of speech was in order to use the foul language of the gutter or of latrine walls. The First Amendment to the United States Constitution was interpreted to mean that such language could not be prohibited (not even in the presence of ladies and of children) and today the surest way to write a best-seller is to string four-letter words together with no ideas in between.

The Ten Commandments were burned in the orgiastic fires of unbridled license. Even preachers (some of them) stood with their own lighted matches. A true preacher of the gospel (at least in the state where I live) became a nuisance to be tolerated but not listened to.

Out of the moral and spiritual chaos emerged the drug culture. The use of hard drugs infiltrated the schools down to the eighth grade. Mind-bending narcotics became the order of the day, and their use was not confined to obscure dives off back alleys, but reached into exclusive homes and into middle-class households.

Alcoholism, once the realm of the older members of society, became the penitentiary of the young. This morning's newspaper carries a headline: "Student Boozing Big in New York." The AP story begins with this lead: "Twelve percent of the city's public, junior and senior high schools are either potential or established alcoholics, a survey disclosed Wednesday."

I was a student in Albuquerque High School during the days of the "Noble Experiment" as it is deridingly called today. I never knew a student who had a pocket flask. How many did you see? I never knew a place where liquor could be bought. Did you? I never worked or traded in a grocery store that sold it; nor any drugstore; nor any sporting goods store. I never ate a meal in a public restaurant where it was available. How about you? I was editor of a small democratic newspaper in 1932 and I kept writing so many editorials against repeal of the Eighteenth Amendment that I got fired. What I wrote by way of argument then has been proven true over and over in the years that have followed.

Do you remember how the "pro" arguments ran? A repetitious one was that with repeal bootlegging and gangsterism would be blotted out. It is true that some bootleggers did go legitimate. The infamous Lewis Rosenthal

did turn his bootlegging enterprise into the Schenly Corporation. The equally notorious Sam Brofman became the
head of Seagrams.

What happened to gangsterism? During World War II
some gangsters were actually let out of prison *to help in the
war effort.* These patriotic gentlemen, kissed on both
cheeks by high ranking government officials (who got a
cut from the deals), turned to bootlegging gasoline stamps;
meat and sugar, also rationed to you and me, were supplied on the black markets controlled by them. What
happened to gangsterism? The Flamingo Hotel in Las
Vegas was started by Bugsy Siegal. (Last Sunday a corps
of California Highway Patrolmen was assigned to and
performed one duty. They conducted the thousands of
cars from the Los Angeles area to the Nevada state line
to see that they obeyed the fifty-five mile per hour speed
limit, imposed, nationally, to save gasoline. Result? A
howl went up that could almost be heard to the Outer
Banks of North Carolina. The casino owners were protesting that the "trade" was so slow in getting there
that there was not enough time left for the suckers to
gamble more than a few million dollars, much of it, according to common belief, skimmed off the top for gang-
ster interests.)

There are simply not enough pages in this little book
to explore the ramifications of the whiskey culture. Besides, to do so, would be simply to parade facts which we
all know too well.

Sexual morality is at an all-time low. The average American city today is simply a twentieth-century Sodom—all
legal-like. Here are two ads published in the *San Jose*

Mercury (San Jose, California, my home). This newspaper serves more than a quarter of a million homes. It is a good newspaper, editorially—one of the best in the nation. Now examine these advertisements, nauseating but completely legal:

"Amateur Nude Couples Dance Contest—every Thursday night at 9:00 PM." This is at a notorious joint in the neighborhood of the church which I pastored twenty-two years. It would have been closed long ago by the district attorney except that *no jury of citizens has yet been impanelled that will sustain the arrests of the proprietors.*

Another ad, same issue, same paper, page 38: "The Regency Lodge, sophistication and privacy. The only hotel showing the latest popular hardcore films on closed circuit TV from 10:00 AM 'til after midnight in the unique atmosphere of rooms done in plush velvet and mirrors with king sized waterbeds." Why cannot the district attorney act against this cesspool within blocks of his own office? He cannot get a jury to convict.

This display advertising is legal in a state where it is illegal for optometrists to advertise eye-glasses at competitive prices. Consequently, my wife last week paid $102 for a pair of ordinary eye-glasses exclusive of the cost of examination (and, of course, Medicare had no part in this).

Continuing the horrible sex story one paragraph. The most unspeakable of all sexual perversions, homosexuality, was unmentioned in polite society when you and I were growing up. Now a sheriff in California can publicly thank the city's homosexuals for his victory margin following his election.

We *do* live in an upside-down world. Some aspects are

for the better. Racism is on the wane. There is a greater
interest in the civil rights of the individual. There are many
other healthy trends which we sincerely applaud. The question faced by people like us is simply: what can I do about
it all? Should I close my eyes and ears and withdraw into
some private hermitage where I can contemplate the sunsets? I do not think so.

One thing we *can* do is to change bad laws. The so-called
senior citizens of this country have enough political clout
to do anything that they choose to do.

There is the grave danger that this political power can be
used in a self-serving way, to gain more material benefits
for ourselves while we bankrupt the young. If we do that,
we are taking on the elements of political gangsterism. On
the other hand we can see that qualified men and women
are elected to public office and we can pray for them and
support them once they are in government. We have voices;
we have influence; we have the time.

We can support the truly democratic way of life. We
believe in America—all of us. What is more, we are proud
of it and do not mind waving the old flag once in awhile.

Our public schools are in deep trouble. Who can save
them? Our children are grown and, for the most part, are
on their own, with their own families to raise. But for the
sake of our beloved grandchildren, and all of the other children of our nation, we can lend our support to the preservation of our schools.

Our churches need our support. Who else on this earth
will teach morality in the light of God's will if the voices
of the churches are silenced?

Our homes are breaking up all over this precious land of

ours? Marriage is threatened. Cohabitation without legal sanction is the order of the day. We can, by example and by tried precept, do our part to save the most divine of all human institutions.

If Paul and Silas could turn their world upside-down (Acts 17:6) then perhaps we can turn our world *right side up.* We cannot bring back the simple days of the Model T, mechanically, economically, sociologically, governmentally, environmentally—the list can span the complexities of our modern lives. We can remind ourselves, however, the Space Age needs to find somewhere in that space, the living Christ and his royal law of love. Then, and only then, can the world know peace.

Let us not seek out our rocking chairs—not just yet. Let us not put our experience, which has given to us a certain needed wisdom, under the cushion of our footstools and forget our obligation to God and to our fellowmen just because we have grown tired of the battle.

7

"The Woman Thou Gavest"

The following story is true. Only the names have been
changed to protect the guilty. My friend Frank retired
some years before I did. Two weeks after he had given
up his job I received a phone call from his wife, Jane. "If
you don't come and get this—this—big oaf away from
here," crackled the line, "I am going to smash my good
electric skillet over his head! Take him away. Take him
anywhere. Just don't be in any hurry to bring him back!"

This domestic crisis—not quite as bad as it sounds—was
provoked by the fact that every time Jane turned around,
Frank was there. When she was in the kitchen, Frank was
in the kitchen. Though he could not have boiled water
without scorching it, he was telling her how to cook. When
she tried to use her electric mixer, he warned her that she
was overloading it (she had only been using it ten years)—
"Them things cost money, you know!"

And while he was on the subject of money, she could save a little—and be patriotic, too—if she turned off the stove burner just a shade before the water boiled and let the residual heat do the job. The refrigerator could be turned down a notch or two, likewise the water heater. ("Got to watch them things; it all adds up.") When Jane tried to vacuum the living room rug, she had actually to pick up Frank's long legs to clean under them. All the time he yelled because she was between a TV touchdown and his eyeballs. So it went. I averted domestic mayhem by showing up there in the nick of time. I proposed that Frank go with me to make some hospital calls in my pastoral capacity. Since he was a deacon, I reminded him, gently, that this was a part of his obligation. By the time we got back the game was over and the Giants had won and the living room was fluffy and clean.

My friend Jane was like the woman who, when asked what she thought of her husband's retirement just said, "Too little money; too much husband." Or like the "ired wife in the retired life syndrome," as described by Dr. John Briggs.

Dr. Briggs, internist of St. Paul, Minnesota, describes the effect upon a woman of good health who suddenly finds that her retired husband is around the house every day. He gets in her way. He interferes with the way she does her work. He is handy with advice. In short, he is just in her hair. Finally she becomes upset, frustrated, antagonistic toward her spouse, and she develops hypochondriacal adjustment mechanisms (pill-popper, I think he means). She gets all manner of aches and pains all derived from a disease called husband (my words).

One such woman revised the marriage contract to read: "For better or worse, but not for lunch." She is not used to fixing a hot lunch every day. She is accustomed to eating a little weight-watcher's salad, turning on the television set to watch her favorite soap opera to see if Ted is really the father of Matilda's unborn child.

Hubby, for Pete's sake, if you value your uncracked skull, make yourself scarce once in awhile, especially at noontime or you are likely to run out of the house one day with your hand on your head and a knot under it yelling so loudly that your neighbors will know that yours is a case of marital incompatability. Do you have a study? Get into it and *stay.* If you don't have one, build it in the attic or in the cellar. Get your own little portable TV so you can watch the white hats murder the black hats and the Pittsburg Steelers fans get drunk. If you have a workshop, get out there and saw your thumb off. If you don't have a workshop, bust the building code and build one on the back of your lot. Do anything that is reasonable and even halfway honorable to get out of your wife's way now and then. The women's libbers are right, up to a point. Your wife does have *some* rights.

My own experience may help some poor, misguided or unguided man. When I took up permanent residence in my home and no longer commuted to the church office, I noticed a number of things that brought me some pain and, at the same time, stimulated my profound admiration, to say nothing of pity, for my little wife.

For instance: I noticed a wooden matchstick wedged in the charger part of her electric knife. When I inquired about this unusual circumstance, I was informed that the match-

stick forced the base of the knife more firmly against
the electrical contacts so the charger would work. She
had told me about the problem about a year before, but
I had put off trying to fix it. I discovered an ingenious
screen on one of the bedroom windows. It was made out
of nylon mesh; and, where you reached through to work
the closer, there was a zipper. Who ever heard of a zipper
on a house window screen? I have, now. I had told her
that it was impossible for me to either buy or make a
screen replacement. Well, I ain't she. Do you know how
her electric hair-dryer works? She had asked me months
before if I could fix it. The idiotic thing would not heat.
I took it apart (and got most of it back together), but
gave up. Since we could not afford another at the time,
I told her that she would just have to stick her head in
the kitchen oven to dry her hair. I came in the other day
and there she sat under the hair-dryer knitting up a storm.
Now it seems that if you hit the base of the thing with
your fist in exactly the right spot it somehow activates
the breaker points on the inside causing them to make
contact *ergo* hot air. *Quod erat demonstrandum* (that's
Latin for "Go soak your head in the rainbarrel"). I had
found that, in addition to being a good cook, my girl was
a mechanical and electrical genius. I found out, too, that
I am expendable.

I decided to assume my neglected role as general handyman. Ina went down to San Diego to visit her mother. As
soon as she was safely on the bus, I rushed home and began
my great project. You see, when I built the house, I put
two big corner windows in the living room. A good part
(too much!) of our time is spent watching the boob tube

so, I took down the floor-length, linen-weave drapes; drew up some plans; bought some walnut-finished plywood; and in a couple of weeks I had built the television set into a corner cabinet which reached up to the bottoms of the windows. On either side of the cabinet, since I had plenty of room, I built nice bookcases complete with antiqued doors.

When my wife came back to town, I met her at the bus station and said, "Have I got a great surprise for you!" We drove up into our driveway and she squeaked, "Where are my drapes?"

I opened the door, and she stood there looking at my built-in cabinet and bookcases for a long time. Then she said, very weakly, "It's nice."

By the way, the drapes are back up. The cabinet is kindling wood. The TV set is back where it used to be, gathering up reflected light from the two corner windows, and I'm still running around the house with my ego busted.

Now, fellows, I learned something. I pass it on to you. A woman will go absolutely crazy if she can't move things around. This part of the female psyche (not the only part!), the easy-going male will never understand. I suppose that every man has had the sad experience of sitting down kerthump on the floor when he failed to notice that his little wife had moved his favorite chair. After such a shattering experience, he learned to look before he sat. Another thing about this furniture moving bit is that the man cannot understand how his weak little wife who could not possibly carry out a sack of garbage can move a grand piano all by herself, if she wants it in the opposite corner. Betty Friedan did not toss this psychological powder-puff around in her book *The Feminine Mystique* (being preoccupied

with the biological); so, this part of the "mystique" will
have to remain misty. Suffice it to say "the hand that rocks
the cradle" slams all the other furniture around, too.

Twenty-four years ago when I built our house, I built
a circulating fireplace that has been my pride and joy. It
took me three long, weary months of hard labor. The
masonry is pretty massive. Inside the house the fireplace,
which is constructed of Arizona sandstone, is seven feet
wide by five feet high. The mantel is of two big slabs of
stone and the hearth is made of three. Outside dimensions
are even larger, sides continuing unbroken two feet above
the comb of the roof.

One day, not too long ago, I caught my wife staring at
that fireplace. She was standing in the center of the room.
A slight frown wrinkled her forehead. "Oh, no, you don't!
That's one thing you are not going to move!" I shouted,
"Hah, hah, hah." The last "hah" was a little weak. I wasn't
so sure.

What I am trying to say, old buddy, is simply this: that
little lady has run that house a long time. If you want to
live happily in retirement—and long—you will let her do it.
It is her way of life and the fact that you are temporarily
at loose ends does not change her life-style except to com-
plicate it by her having to step over the omnipresent you.
She must keep her independence. And she'll never outgrow
this need. My little mother-in-law, presented earlier in these
pages, has her own small apartment in San Diego. She
would be welcome to live with any of her children—and
four of them are in California, but her answer is a firm, "I
want to boss my own dishrag." Exactly.

Husbands in their self-pity are likely to forget that their

wives have troubling mental adjustments to make, too.
Sometimes their battle is greater than ours. You and I
can fight back against being removed from general circulation; they really have no way to do so. They are tied to
our shadow. One day the husband is a Somebody. He is
an achiever. He is looked up to and respected. He is a
productive member of the social structure, no matter what
his job. He pays taxes. He is Mr. Citizen, first class. The
next day he is Mr. Nobody. He is not a name but a nine-
digit number. His wife is Mrs. 564-64-1004. She has
become the wife of a nobody without even getting di-
vorced. She needs more love than you gave her on your
honeymoon; more understanding and consideration even
than you gave her when she went down into the valley
and presented you with your firstborn.

Don't forget that while your situation has been changed
radically, hers, physically, has been altered less. She is
forced to continue in the same way, doing the things that
she has always done. Unless she has held a job herself, she
has never had to punch a time clock; she will not now.
Moreover, she is now required to manage the house on half
the budget at a time when prices are spiraling astronomi-
cally. She comes back from the supermarket with fifty
dollars worth of groceries in one paper bag and with a look
of utter exhaustion on her face. She is a casualty of the
battle of the pushcarts where other women shoppers
scramble and clutch to save two cents on a single item.
This is about the only way her dreary routine has changed,
and it is for the worse.

And then, my friend, there is you—in living color—all
the time. You are wondering what to do with yourself, and

she is wondering what to do with you. You see, up to this point in your married life you have lived together just *part* of the time. Every day at a certain hour you have gone off to work with her warm kiss still lingering on your lips, and you have returned in the evening to a wifely hug and kiss and a hot dinner—maybe with *steak!* But at least you have been gone about one third of the time. You may think that I am just trying to be funny. I devoutly wish that it were so. I have counseled with enough older women to know that this problem is poignantly real. Recognizing that the difficulty is real is the first step toward alleviating it. Our male egos may suffer just a bit, but our wives, during our retirement, do not need us underfoot all the time.

This is not to say that a husband should refuse to do any housework. The ordinary pastor and his wife solved this problem many years ago. He admitted to himself that she carried her full load of church responsibilities, went with him in his rounds of visitation every day; in short, she was an unpaid worker in the church. Therefore, he shared the household responsibilities with his helpmate, and he did it cheerfully. In the old days I never knew a pastor who was not an expert dish-drier (D.D.). I could dry, when I was at my best, five dinner plates at a time without touching my grimy paws to any! That, after all, is a *man's* job. Did you ever see any biblical reference to a woman's drying a dish? Now, look up 2 Kings 21:13, King James Version. I used to sell that information to housewives at two-bits a whack, when I was a ministerial student in college. As I say, most pastors are already housebroken but it should not be beneath the dignity of any real man to help his beloved now and then with *her* tasks—provided, of course, that she wants him to.

Now, with that all cleared up, let us get to the most serious consideration of all: the right of any woman to personhood. This idea spearheads the women's equal rights movements, called by whatever name. I have no sympathy whatsoever with the segment of women's lib who insist on tacking the title "Ms." to their names. To me, it sounds like a mosquito buzzing. I usually want to swat one, but most of them look tougher than I do, and they scare the living daylights out of me. I suppose that my antipathy stems from the fact that I believe that to be a wife and mother is the highest calling for any woman. I know that I sound like what the Mz-z-z-s's call a "male chauvinist pig." I deny that, heatedly. Who ever heard of a pig named "Harold"? It is usually "Arnold." I looked up that word "chauvinist" in Brother Noah Webster's big book that keeps on changing the subject. He says that a chauvinist is a jingoist. I ran that rabbit into its hole and it said that a jingoist is one who influences by jingoism. I won't even admit that I am a porcine jingoist.

Now that I have freely admitted my old-fashioned prejudice, I come back to insist that any woman, married or not, has a God-given right to be her own person. In order to find self-expression, many women have taken careers which, they feel, have given them a sense of worth and accomplishment. At the same time they have been homemakers. Theirs has been a double task, and I do not minimize it nor downgrade it. The career woman faces the trauma of retirement even as does any other productive member of the social order.

Putting this all together, is not the period of retirement a time for self-realization—for men; for women? There are so many ways in which we can find identity. The opportunities are not limited to life vocations. Perhaps, in retirement, we can, for the first time in our entire lives, be free to choose and to follow the desires of our hearts.

Husband—Wife—if God has in his grace given you these golden years together you will find them to be the sweetest you have ever known.

Widows—Unmarried—your way may be harder and the path may be rougher (not always!), but the gift of life is yours. The sunrises will be lovelier, the sunsets more beautiful, and the hours more precious than you have ever dreamed. Meet tomorrow confidently.

8
Eyes in the Wilderness

I leaned my backpack against the trunk of a scarred
and weatherbeaten old pine and sat down on a rock crop-
ping at the eight-thousand foot level of the John Muir
Trail through the Sierras. Below me stretched the vast
Emigrant Basin wilderness area bounded on all sides by
towering, ragged peaks which gave the range its name
(Saws). I was on my way up above timberline to the
golden trout country and my aluminum-cased-fly-rod rode
on the top of the pack, unjointed to a length of eighteen
inches. A goose-down sleeping bag rode easily at the
bottom.

In this part of the Basin, under the trail, the timber
stood in patches; pine, some fir, and western red cedar.
Thickets of willow and wild lilacs choked the trickling
watercourses, deep in the canyon. High overhead a hawk
circled, and a lone white cloud wandered by like a sheep

lost from the vanished herd. I sucked in my breath. God had grown lavish—almost careless—here, as he scattered beauty over the rugged land as wantonly as a child throws away handfuls of flower petals. No sound was heard—at first. I closed my eyes and sat for long moments half asleep.

Then from the meadow down, and slightly to my right I heard a sharp noise like the cracking of a snow-laden limb in the winter night. I looked quickly. Two mighty mule deer bucks were fighting. Their antlers looked like rocking-chairs as they charged together like battering rams. The antlers hung up, and the bucks shook them loose and backed away from each other. I whipped up my eight-power binoculars and focused them with one rapid twist of the center wheel. The combatants charged again. There was another crack as of a limb yielding to the wind. Again they backed off, sizing each other up, warily, then crack! The sound ricocheted off the rocks and reached my ears.

While I watched with wonder, the tremendous animals, either of which would have weighed more than two hundred pounds, charged again and again. I could not understand how their heads could take such shattering punishment. My own ached just from watching. Six times—I counted them—the bucks smashed together. Finally one turned, and with a final shake of his antlered head, vanished around a rock. The victor stood for a moment, snorting and pawing like an angry bull. Then he leisurely walked over to join his harem, eight sleek, beautiful does. They had gone on browsing on the tender wild lilac twigs and leaves, seemingly unconcerned about the outcome of the battle.

A vagrant thought crossed my mind. I pulled it back and examined it while I continued to rest. The night before, at our cabin in the Sonora Pass country, I had read my Bible readings for the day and the verses flashed now in my mind's eye.

Two strong men were butting their heads together, not actually, but figuratively. The wanderers of the Exodus were breaking camp to resume their journey to the Promised Land. Standing apart from the bustle and commotion, Moses and Hobab were saying good-bye to each other. It was then that they hit head-on. This was no contest of bucks over does—men for women. Hobab was the father-in-law of Moses. His daughter may have entered the picture, but certainly not as a prize. She was already won. Moses was offering to Hobab not women, but wealth—prized by some soulless men even more.

Moses made a proposition that few men could have refused: "We are journeying unto the place of which the Lord said, 'I will give it you.' Come thou with us, and we will do thee good." Today the argument would run something like this: "You come with us and I'll cut you in on a good deal. There is land in Canaan just for the taking. It has grass for the herds, water for the fields. You can pull the dollars right off the trees, and you won't have to worry about a tax shelter because there are no income taxes. Everything will be ours. You can't turn down a deal like this. Get with it!"

Hobab just looked at him. Then he said, quietly: "I will not go. I will depart to mine own land, and to mine own kindred."

The Israelite leader blinked his eyes in disbelief. Then he

took a new measure of the man before him. Hobab was an old sheik of the desert. His skin was wind-burned leather. His eyes had gathered up twenty-thousand sunsets. They flashed, now, with their own fire. Moses, too, was a master of men. Here the two powerful sheiks were face to face, but not mind with mind. No man who ever lived was stronger than Moses. His every word was law and was to be obeyed without question. Only rarely was he defied, and then, his antagonists paid dearly for their folly. But here was a man with an unbending will of his own. That will of steel was forged in the crucibles of the desert sun, tempered by the winds which blew from the tops of snow-capped mountains. He had been with this motley crowd long enough to note their confusion, to sense their fear and uncertainty. Before them lay no traveled roads where they could put their feet with confidence.

It was as though Moses could read the mind of Hobab. This is a quality of leadership. He realized, as he studied the face of the other, that he had committed a foolish offense. This man needed absolutely nothing that he, nor his followers, could offer. "Come thou with us and we will do thee good"—it was a bonehead play. It was little short of being insulting.

Quickly, then, as a good leader would, Moses changed his ploy. He spoke, and his long whiskers moved with the shaping of his words. There was now a note of pleading. It was genuine; no faking here. The invitation was the exact opposite to what it had been before: "Leave us not, I pray thee; for as much as thou knowest how we are to encamp in the wilderness, and thou mayest be to us instead of eyes." The argument, though unspoken, was:

Hobab, we need *you;* I need you. You know the desert
as few others do. You know where the water lies hidden
under the rocks. You know the easiest way to pick a trail
over the mountains. You know the haunts of lions and the
wild animals which can threaten our flocks and even our
children. You have been over much of the ground before.
You can *see* where we can only guess. Come, I beg you,
come. *Be our eyes,* then we can see.

In my imagination I could see Moses walk over and lay
a hand on the shoulder of the stalwart man who faced
him, and who had, so far, won in this battle of the minds
and wills. He looked long into the eyes of the other.

Then, without another word; without one look backward, old Hobab became a wanderer with the others. He
had responded to the call to the best that was within himself.

* * *

Probably, Hobab, had he been employed by the Mt.
Sinai Mining Corporation, would, long since, have been
handed his self-winding watch, and his Medicare card and
been told, "Get lost." There would probably have been
the explanation, "We gotta have guys with muscle."

Well, Hobab *did* have some muscle left—enough to conquer the wilderness where younger men lay down and
died. What was more important than physical strength
was his knowledge, gained through the years, and the wisdom to make good use of that knowledge, gained
through experience.

* * *

Let us bring this home to our own hearts and lives. You
and I, all through our adult lives, have been the "eyes" of

wisdom to someone else. We have shown the way; we have blazed the trail. They have walked in our footprints.

One evening, in the long ago, I lay on the living room sofa reading the paper. Suddenly there was a pull at my hair, a snip of scissors, and my tiny son, barely three years old, had appropriated something that he did not need—a part of my hair. (He was playing barber.) Needless to say, I came alive with a wild yell that could have been heard all the way down to Main Street. My toddler tried to run toward the bedroom, but tripped and fell over his own feet. You see, he had not only appropriated some of my hair, but he had also taken to himself my hunting boots. When he tried to run, he tripped. One boot flew one way and the scissors slithered across the floor in another direction.

"What are you doing with my boots?" I shouted, as he scrambled to his feet.

"I was jus' wearing boots," he said, as, with one boot left on, he tried again for the hall door.

I jerked off my bedroom slipper and just as he made the doorway, I threw it at him. I still remember that beautiful shot! I took him right square on the bottom of his funny-looking pants. Then I followed him into the bedroom, undressed him, and put him in his small bed. As I tucked him in for the night, the thought hit me almost like a bullet: If Leland was going to walk in my boots, I'd better be careful where I wore them. He is today sitting at the city desk of the Los Angeles Times. He is Assistant Metropolitan Editor of perhaps the greatest newspaper in the world (at least he says that it is).

I am not trying to walk in the shadow of my own son, but I say that, had I once walked into the gutter, he might have followed me there.

Yes; you and I have been the "eyes" to many people. Sometimes we did not know it. Here is another leaf from my memory book:

I was the featured speaker for a youth assembly at Inlow Youth Camp in the scenic Manzano Mountains of New Mexico. The camp was named for one of the greatest Christians I have ever known—Miss Eva Inlow.

This particular night, after the service, I had started walking toward my tent, pitched under the towering pines along a hiking trail. I could hardly see my way, for the only light was that of the stars. Suddenly I was grabbed from behind. To say that I was startled is to understate the situation. I was plain scared.

Then a voice spoke in my ear. It was the voice of a youth in his early teens. He simply said, "Thank you for what you have done for me" and melted into the trees and the black night. I never saw his face; I never heard his name. I had no idea just what I had done for the youth, and I never found out. One thing is certain: my unknown young friend, probably ashamed to show his emotion in daylight, wanted me to know that somehow, if for a moment, I had been "eyes" for him along the wilderness trail of life.

You, too, have influenced, for the better, countless people, young and old and *you never knew it.* You were their "eyes" that saw the better way.

Here is a strange paradox. As we grow older, our physical eyes grow dimmer, but the older we get the further we see with our spiritual eyes. Their vision is not dimmed.

What greater blessing could we possibly know than to

be the "eyes" of the young?

Please meet Edwin and Alva Hollinger. They were members of First Baptist Church, Las Cruces, New Mexico, when I became its pastor. I was twenty-seven—both young and foolish. They took me under their wings as did Aquila and Priscilla with young Apollos to whom they, most considerately, I am sure, "expounded unto him the way of God more perfectly." (They were my "eyes.")

Edwin, for some reason I do not know, was called "Scout." I liked that. The name suited him perfectly. Webster defines "scout" as "one who keeps a lookout." That is—one who sees. A scout is also a pioneer. Moffatt translates Hebrews 12:2, "our eyes fixed upon Jesus as the *pioneer.*" He could as well have said "scout."

One day as deacon Hollinger and I ripped along the highway toward Albuquerque (he always drove just about a foot *above* the road), he turned his eyes toward me and asked: "How are your debts? Do you owe any money?"

I was a little flustered. "I guess that I owe a total of one hundred dollars."

Scout Hollinger spun the car to the side of the road. He took out his checkbook and wrote a check in my name for one hundred dollars. "Take that and pay your debts. I know that you don't get much salary, but it won't do for our pastor to owe a lot of unpaid bills."

I protested, "But I don't know when I will be able to pay this back."

"If you ever get one hundred dollars and have no place to put it, pay it back. Otherwise, forget it," answered Hollinger.

That has been forty years ago. So far, I have never had

that much money with no place to put it.

Hollinger was then in the State Extension Service at New Mexico A. and M. College—now New Mexico State University. The Hollinger home was just off campus. It was there that we organized one of the first of all Baptist Student Unions. From then until now Edwin and Alva Hollinger have kept young by being interested in, and associated with college students.

To continue the story of this dedicated couple, I must digress briefly. When I became pastor of the Las Cruces church, it was depression times. The church had a beautiful new brick building but had defaulted on its payments with the result that the house of worship was up for sale to the highest bidder. I got that set aside long enough to go down to Abilene, Texas, to interview a Christian businessman named W. J. Behrens. He had given many thousands of dollars to Hardin-Simmons University, there. We needed $16,000 to save our building and had raised among the members $3,000. I asked Mr. Behrens to lend us the rest. He refused flatly. Later, as we walked across the University campus, he confided with pride, "I have put two hundred students through this school.."

Don't you see? He had been the "eyes" to these young people. Through his eyes, they, too, could see the future. (Later, two of my own daughters attended college there working their way through. They fell in love with, and married two ministerial students, who were classmates.)

Midway across the campus, Mr. Behrens stopped and put his hand on my shoulder. He looked into my eyes for a long moment, then said, "You are very young. I am more interested in helping *you* than I am in lending money to your church." The upshot was that he did lend the money—with the proviso that our members take out that amount in life insurance with the company which he headed. (He also made me promise that I would stay with the church until the loan was retired. I did—ten years.)

The Hollingers invested all the money that they could spare in insurance on Alva's life—mainly to help our church.

Twenty-nine years passed. By that time the Hollingers, my wife and I, were living in California. It had long been the vision of this couple that a student union building be constructed near New Mexico State. Word came that the New Mexico Baptist State Mission Board had agreed to the building of the center at a cost of $100,000 if $30,000 could be made available as a down payment. The Hollingers pulled their trailer back to New Mexico and traveled over the state raising the money. They gave several thousand dollars themselves. Finally the down payment was in hand but by that time inflation had reared its ugly head and $10,000 more was needed. They borrowed on their insurance policies and provided this as a loan. Now, follow that $10,000.

When they moved to California, they were accompanied by Alva's sister, Beth, and her husband, Gordon Chilton. These, too, had been faithful members of the Las Cruces First Baptist Church. They bought homes in Vista, near San Diego. They immediately found that the new church, with which they had affiliated, Buena Vista Baptist, was in a building program. Since the New Mexico State Mission Board had repaid their loan, they made the $10,000 available to their church.

In due time the church repaid the loan. California Bap-

tist College in Riverside, furnished the Hollingers with another opportunity to be of service to young people. (I know
what happened because I was a trustee of the college.) The
college needed desperately to enlarge its library facilities,
so the Hollingers again released the $10,000 for this pur-
pose. At the insistence of the trustees, the new addition
was named "The Hollinger Periodical Wing." To date this
devoted couple has given more than $20,000 to the insti-
tution, according to its business manager, J. L. Harden.

Again Scout Hollinger and his gracious wife, Alva, had
been "eyes" to youth.

An interesting sidelight which came out of my interview
with these old friends was the fact that they had supported
financially and otherwise, Montezuma Baptist College, my
own alma mater, lost to Baptists during the depression.

The Hollingers are not wealthy people. How, then, were
they able to do all this? Edwin Hollinger is now eighty-
two; his wife, Alva, is seventy-seven. At the comparatively
young age of fifty-seven, Hollinger was retired because of
a heart ailment. Listen to their explanation:

"In the early years of the twentieth century with no Social Security or annuity or retirement systems we saw many
older people (over sixty-five) dependent on others for their
subsistence. We were glad to be able to help our parents
and others of their generation with living expenses. We had
no desire to be wealthy but felt determined to provide for
ourselves. So we set up our own retirement plan by setting
aside at least ten percent of our little income in addition
to ten percent for our church and charities." He also said,
significantly, "We lived thriftily."

Edwin and Alva Hollinger can look backward to the days

when our country was relatively unspoiled, with its air clean and its streams sparkling and pure. They look about them in the smog-filled Los Angeles basin where they live and their eyes smart and their heads hurt. Everywhere, as they travel, they see the rape of our precious land by uncaring individuals. They know that the America of the future is doomed unless someone—many someones—begin to care and to do something about it.

A recent letter from them includes this statement:

"Conservation has always been Edwin's profession and will continue to be because the principles and practice of conservation are essential to the survival of our country. Our recycling efforts have been done to demonstrate what many people can do in stopping the waste and pollution problems at their source (the home), and the preservation of needed materials for our nation now and for the oncoming generations. We cooperate with the local grade school that uses conservation at the home level as an educational project.

Thus the Hollingers are still being "eyes in the wilderness" for the young.

Now let me toss into the warm nest of our complacency a mental bombshell. We, who are Social Security pensioners, are the only people ever, in the entire history of the world, *to be paid not to work!*

We should be able to give to the society which makes this possible, a little of our time.

What, then, can we do?

Perhaps my conversation with a dedicated young man last night will tell us something. We talked until almost eleven o'clock.

I had noticed a writeup by a columnist of the *San Jose
Mercury,* named Leigh Weimers, which I quote. Since the
teacher involved is on the faculty of the high school where
my grandson Kenny was a member of the football team
and my granddaughter Cary is a member of the band, I
felt free to phone the young man involved in the story. I
had meant to confine my interview to the telephone, but
he said that he would be glad to come by my house—such
is his dedication to the program outlined and conceived by
him.

Here is what the column said:

"Up bright and early this Monday for the wearin' of
the green (or, in a recession, "barren of the green"),
we come to no one brighter or earlier than Don Rogers.
(The column, as you may have guessed, appeared on
St. Patrick's Day, 1975.)

"Rogers, a bountifully bearded Del Mar High
teacher, has an idea which already is getting raves at
the highest levels of government.

" 'The response has been almost totally enthusiastic,'
he says enthusiastically. 'What we'd like to do is make
sure the knowledge amassed by one generation is
passed on to the next by having Senior Citizens come
into the classrooms and share their experience with the
students.'

"A beautifully simple idea, not to mention being
simply beautiful.

" 'There's a lot of talent out there not being appre-
ciated,' Rogers continues. 'Our older people have a
wealth of vocational know-how, skills in handiwork
that might otherwise be lost, and expertise in a wide

variety of subjects. If we can get them together with
our young people, it could improve our culture nation-
wide, give our elderly the respect they deserve, and en-
liven education. Just because a teacher is young
doesn't mean he necessarily has young ideas, you know.'

"What's needed now is to see if the Senior Citizens
share the same enthusiasm as the educational and
governmental brass, Rogers says."

* * *

This young high school teacher is trying with all his
might to get a program underway that can reach throughout our nation. It can revolutionize some of our educational concepts. It can most certainly help to bridge the
so-called generation gap. It can increase the confidence of
the general public in our public schools.

Surely such a program can help the retiree to be of service, and, concomitantly, can restore to him a sense of dignity and worth—if he, or she—has lost it.

This program is in the embryonic stage at present. It has
not been funded—yet, though, I feel confident it will be.
Don Rogers is a high school teacher (sociology) full-time.
There is no organization, no personnel as yet. The fact is,
though, that each of us, no matter where he lives, can become associated with a similar effort.

The unspoken cry of youth, today, as never before, is
"Leave us not. You know the way through the wilderness
of life. Be our eyes."

A well-known poem comes to my mind. Long ago, I
wrote it on my heart. I can now write it on paper without
looking it up—though I'll probably get the punctuation
wrong.

The Bridge Builder

An old man, going on a lonely way,
Came at the evening, cold and gray,
To a chasm vast and deep and wide;
The old man crossed in the twilight dim,
The sullen stream had no fear for him;
But he turned when safe on the other side
And built a bridge to span the tide.
"Old man," said a fellow-pilgrim near,
"You are wasting your strength with building here;
Your journey will end with the ending day,
You never again will pass this way;
You've crossed the chasm deep and wide,
Why build a bridge to span the tide?"
The builder lifted his old gray head—
"Good friend, in the path I have come," he said,
"There followeth after me today
A youth whose feet must pass this way.
This chasm that has been naught to me,
To that fair-haired youth may a pitfall be;
He, too, must cross in the twilight dim;
Good friend, I am building this bridge for him."

—Selected

9

"Come...Rest Awhile"

My wife will never make a fisherperson. Her first word on the subject was during our honeymoon; her last was just a few days ago. A new acquaintance asked her, "Do you fish?"

With that deceptively sweet voice of hers belying the glint in her eyes she said, "No, I don't fish."

"Why not?" asked the curious one, and I instinctively ducked.

"Because," said my Beloved, "fifty years ago I caught a sucker. That was enough for me."

Now if you happen to be an ichthylogical egghead, my wife was not referring to *Pantosteus platyrhynous*. She meant *me*.

My wife and I were married while we were students in Montezuma Baptist College in New Mexico. This was strictly against college regulations. Montezuma was six miles north of Las Vegas, in the Sangre de Cristo Mountains. Male and female students were (presumably) kept separated almost entirely by restrictive rules. At church services on Sunday the boys sat on one side of the auditorium and the girls on the other. They were allowed to visit at "social hour" Friday evenings, always with a long-nosed, telescopic-eyed, banjo-eared chaperone monitoring the affair. Since the only way you could be with your girl was to marry her, many of the boys did just that. One year in this small college of a few more than one hundred students, there were eight marriages. Back home the mothers began to howl in protest. The faculty and president sat up all night and formulated some decrees: students who married during the school term would lose their credits for that term and would be suspended from school. If I remember correctly, there were only seven weddings the next year, one of which was ours. The president of the college, Dr. C. R. Barrick, still living, performed our marriage ceremony, then expelled us the next morning for getting married. I never held it against him. In fact, I love him as I do few men on the earth.

Our friend, Pablo Padilla, offered us his adobe cabin up on the turbulent Gallinas River for our honeymoon. The trouble was, the Gallinas was then, and perhaps still is, a good rainbow trout stream.

One afternoon I shouldered my willow basket creel, took my fly rod in one hand and my bride's hand in my other and we crossed the Gallinas on rocks jutting up from a shallow place in the stream's bed. We went up a neighboring canyon where a small tributary creek meandered down to spread itself now and then into reasonably deep

pools caught behind beaver dam weirs. In one of those
pools I saw the dark, shadowy forms of good-sized trout.
I soon flicked a royal coachman over the water and let it
settle down without a splash. Then a twelve-incher made
the water boil in a vicious strike. Bride, honeymoon, and
all else was forgotten as I played that iridescent beauty to
the net. Before I could cast again, it started to rain, and,
brother if you ain't seen rain in the Sangre de Cristos, you
ain't seen rain nowhere!

Then my little wife did an absolutely senseless, unbe-
lievable thing. With fish like those ready to be had, she
yelled, "Let's get out of here!" I know you will find that
hard to believe but that's exactly what she did.

With my wife protesting and yelling like the thunder
rolling off Hermit's Peak up above us, I calmly changed
over from a fly to a worm. Before you could say "incom-
patibility," I had hooked another trout. Then another.
And another. The rain came down in sheets. I caught
twelve fish.

To shorten this bittersweet episode, I finally heeded
the howling anguish of my new wife, and started back
with her. Besides, I had my limit of fish by then, anyway.

When we got back to the place where we had crossed
over the Gallinas, it was running bank to bank with roar-
ing, muddy water. I had to wade that icy water up to my
chest and carry my wife across. Then about halfway to
the other side that fool girl—I mean my precious darling—
somehow dropped my creel which she was holding because
I was holding her, into that flood, and it was swept away.
She murmured in my ear, "I'm so sorry." I should have
pitched her in after the creel, but by then I was hungry

and didn't know how to cook.

About twenty-five years later I decided that the best way to jerk one leg off the domestic triangle (my wife, the fish, and I) was to insist that she catch at least one fish, then she would be "hooked." We then had a cabin at Ruidoso, New Mexico. One day we went up the Ruidoso ("noisy") River into the Mescalero-Apache Indian reservation where I found the big pool that had been so productive for me in years gone by. I had bought a fishing license for Ina so I rigged up my brand-new split-bamboo fly-rod with my new automatic reel and tapered fly line and handed it to her. I said, as I led her out on to a huge rock jutting out into the pool, "Watch me and do exactly what I do and you will catch a fish."

I went upstream about fifty yards and began to cast out over the water with my old fly-rod. In a moment I heard a shrill scream. I looked around just in time to see my wife, my new fly-rod, and all disappear into the ice-cold water. They went completely out of sight.

I ran back to the deep pool and got my new fly-rod and new automatic reel out of the water. Then I got my wife out. I took her down to the cabin and dried her off and said, "That's it."

But it wasn't. After that I almost got her and myself drowned in Elephant Butte Lake when a sudden storm came up and waves came over the boat, swamping it. We finally got to the shore ourselves, but we never saw the boat or any of its contents again. I tried once more before I finally gave up. Off Moss Landing, in California, we were almost swept out to sea when my little three and one-half horsepower outboard motor could not conquer the windblown waves.

My wife does not fish nor hunt, but I really do not care. She can *cook* the fish I catch and serve them up with such a delectable flavor that you dream about it. She can cook a venison roast to the ultimate in perfection. She can take one of our old black Dutch ovens (we have two of them) and produce a culinary masterpiece that would make the head chef of the Waldorf-Astoria look like a tenderfoot Boy Scout struggling with a "hunter's twist."

Although I gave up trying to make a fisherperson out of Ina (I never did try to make a hunter out of her though she can shoot either a big-game rifle or heavy revolver with ease and accuracy), we both like to hike and camp. The call of the wilderness country is strong within us. I can never get her so far back into the primitive places that she is the least bit afraid—the wilder it is, the better she likes it!

We have a four-wheel drive Scout International. It could climb a tree—almost. I took the back seat out, built two plywood boxes with piano-hinge lids, the width of the vehicle and ten inches deep. Fit end to end they make a platform for a deep, rubber foam mattress. In one of the boxes (the rear one) we keep stored a gasoline stove, nest of good cooking and eating utensils, including the smaller of the Dutch ovens, big iron skillet and other necessities for cooking. In this box, also, are shovel, machete, miner's pick and rockhound hammer, gallon Thermos jug, Safari light, mechanic's tools, cans of lubricating oil, transmission and brake fluids, anti-freeze, thirty-foot tow chain with a separate ten foot length, each with heavy steel clevis hooks— all kinds of heavier items. In the other box are: nylon tent, sleeping bags, curtains that snap into place around the car windows for privacy, two air mattresses, folding chairs and table, tablecloths—all lighter things. Over the wheel well a four-foot-long 6,000-pound capacity "Handyman" jack insures that we can get out of almost any off-road difficulty (when you're stuck in four-wheel drive, you are *stuck*). Of course we have *four* sturdy tire chains and other odds and ends fitted in beside the boxes.

We can—and do—sleep in some of the most beautiful bedrooms that God has ever made. We can sit under mountain or desert stars by a quietly burning campfire, saying nothing to break the silence, just enjoying being close to God and to each other.

We like to battle the storms together, pitting our lesser strength against the elements. At least there is no smog in a high country snowstorm. Actually the only times that we really enjoy the out-of-doors are: spring, summer, fall, and winter.

Ina gathers up pieces of glass which have been turned by the desert sun into beautiful purple and from them fashions gorgeous hanging lampshades. She uses a big beach ball as a sort of inverse mold, makes the scalloped shade out of resin, sets the many colored pieces of glass from as many places, into lovely patterns, and gives the finished product to loved ones. Several of her works of art adorn our home. I live in fear that she will reach under a desert shrub some time and get a rattlesnake's fangs in her pretty hand. She knows the risk and gladly assumes it. She is an artist with driftwood. What I am saying is that she, too, has hobbies that interest her, and allow her self-expression. We both have excellent cameras and know how to use them. We have rock-polishing equipment—our interests are wide in scope.

We can forget our cares and drop our worries like heavy knapsacks when we can get out into the wild places. Our camps have taken us coast to coast many times, to Canada, and to the tip of Baja California to Cabo San Lucas, to most of the national parks; I have fished the Atlantic, the Pacific, the Gulf of Mexico near Corpus Christi, the Sea of Cortez, the Great Lakes, in Canada, in the Bering Straits and the Arctic Ocean—and once in awhile I have even caught a fish!

Up to this time I have had to fish with a pole in one hand and a watch in the other, so to speak. I have had to hunt with a wary eye fixed on the calendar to see that I did not overstay my time. We have been slaves (as, have you) to the ticking moments. Now it is different. We can stay where we please (as long as it is practically free)—as long as we please. That means that we can live next-door to heaven.

* * *

The thing that turns me on, though, may leave you cold as a frozen mackerel. I am not trying to suggest that you become a fisherman (pardon the generic term). Neither would I hint that you should learn to shoot and hunt in this day when to eat beef is a virtue and to eat venison is a vice. These pursuits have been in my own background— and that makes a difference!—they were a part of my boy- hood culture. I was six or seven years old when I sat on the lap of the notorious outlaw, Henry Starr, and with his hand wrapped around my tiny one, shot his heavy-caliber revolver. This was in Tahlequah, Oklahoma. Starr and his wife lived, briefly, two blocks from my home. I am as much Cherokee as was Will Rogers. I deny that I like to

hunt because I am cruel by nature; I deny that I like guns
because I feel that I am sexually inadequate (as the anti-gun
people jeeringly like to say). I think that I could rationally
explain my feelings, but there is little point in my doing so.
What I am trying to do, however, is to sustain the point
that we *all* need to use our leisure time in ways deeply satisfying to ourselves.

Some hobbies are the outgrowth of a lifetime. They are
almost instinctive and do not need to be learned by us for
the waning years. We have practiced them too long. We
are experts. Other hobbies can be learned.

Our friends of many years, Forrest and Ileta Johnson,
took up work in ceramics when he retired. Forrest was
a carpenter—and a good one. I liked to watch him work.
His smooth, swift movements were a kind of physical
poetry. He is also something of a mechanical genius. He
saw, in an encyclopedia, the picture of an early eighteenth-
century weaving loom. From that picture alone, he constructed a counterpart. It is so large that it fills one end
of his workshop. On this loom he can weave beautiful
rugs. He made his own knitting machine on which he
knits mechanically, socks and stockingcaps, sweaters and
dresses—anything that can be made out of yarn.

Ileta hates fish and fishing. She is orthodox in her belief—up to a point. She believes that God created man
and woman and all living things—except fish. The devil
created fish. Just to mention fish in her presence causes
her skin to break out in a rash. I am persuaded that it
would have been a sinful waste of time for me ever to have
put a fishing pole in Ileta's hands. On the other hand, both
she and Forrest are experts in ceramics. This is a craft that

they have learned solely after retirement. Forrest built an
addition to their house where they have working tables and
kilns. From this shop they turn out a variety of beautifully decorated pieces, each fashioned with patient, loving
care. They sell a few treasures at Christmastime, but their
main objective is to be at work, at an absorbing hobby.

Golf is something else that can be of endless pleasure
and can supply both mental and physical relaxation. The
skills of this fascinating game can be learned, at least to
the point of reasonable proficiency, after the age of retirement. Here, I am not speaking from my own experience.
I do not know one golf club from another. I never wanted
to shoot a birdie unless I could eat it. I wish that I had
taken up the sport. I, at least, could have had a greater
fellowship with my pastor friends, except that I suspect
them, one and all, of being liars. (Fishermen do not lie.)

I do not have to be a golfing enthusiast to appreciate
a phrase which occurred over and over in the books on
retirement which I have read. Certain retirees were described as "playing golf with frenzy." The writers pictured
golfers, who, having reached the age of retirement, felt
that they just *had* to spend infinite hours on a golf course—
not because they wanted to, but because they had been
telling themselves for years that this would be their supreme
joy when the golden days of retirement came around. These
unfortunates had turned what was once a delightful past-
time into a driving compulsion. This, of course, defeats
the very purpose of recreation.

Many thousands of retirees get great enjoyment out of
full-time trailering, drifting along where they want to go,
seeing new faces, gathering different experiences, learning

about their country. A surprisingly large number of these enthusiasts are widows and single women—so many, in fact, that the largest of the trailering magazines, *Trailer Life,* to which I subscribe and which I read avidly, has an interesting column called "Woman Alone." There are trailering clubs with thousands of chapters scattered across the country. One of the largest of these is the "Good Sam" club, sponsored by the before-mentioned magazine. The name, as you have recognized, comes from the story of the Good Samaritan, of the book of Luke. This is, indeed, a fascinating life for those who are able to accept it.

By far the majority of trailerites are those who use their trailers part time. Many retirees sell their homes, purchase mobile homes, and travel trailers, and roam the land at will knowing that in their absence their property will be looked after.

This could continue into a compendium of hobbies and pleasureful pursuits, but there is little point in such a catalogue. What is more to the point is to admit to ourselves that after a lifetime of hard work a little idleness is not a sin. We need not feel guilty when we gather to ourselves a full measure of pleasure in these remaining years. In doing so we shall live longer, but what is more, we shall add to the life we live, a better quality.

* * *

John the Baptist was dead. He had dared to be a man. His head rolled at the feet of a godless woman, her wanton daughter, and a spineless puppet king.

The disciples gathered the body of the rugged man of the desert and buried him. Then they sought out Jesus and told him what had happened.

Jesus, with his own heart like lead within him, lifted up his hands, not yet pierced with the nails, and said to those in the brotherhood of broken hearts, "Come ye yourselves apart into a desert place, and rest awhile."

It was a sweet invitation, and they tried to accept it, but, as you will remember, the crowds outran them to the desert. There was no rest in the face of corporate need.

How many times has this happened to you, in your life of Christian service? You have wanted some rest but you could not. Someone in need was always there. Someone was pulling at you to give more and more of yourself. You, too, have wanted to cry, but you could not. You were the Leader; you were Strength; you were Serenity; you were everything capitalized except YOU.

I know.

Now, at last, there comes a time when we can accept the call of Jesus. We can go somewhere with him, to some lonely place, to the desert, as he invited them, to the mountain where he went when the crowds, with their full bellies were gone, to the seashore where his spirit soared . . . we can find some measure of quietness for ourselves.

Can there be any wrong; can there be any guilt in that? Not unless God, himself, were wrong. And that is unthinkable.

If recreation would do for us what the word says— re-create us—then we must walk with our Creator. We must be in his hands. And I somehow feel that we must do it without effort, without much thinking about it.

After our own refreshment, we can feed others, and nothing is said in this book about retiring *from* our fellowmen. We could not do it, if we chose.

It is to say that we owe something to ourselves. Let us pay that debt before the books close—too soon.

Take a little rest, however you can find it.

10

"I Will Lift Up Mine Eyes"

It was a whispery sort of day. A brooding silence lay over the desert sands, and if it was broken at all, the sound was muted, apologetic. On the roughest part of the Judean hillsides, where the water had been stayed from its rush down to the sand below, flame-colored flowers winked and nodded from the rock crevices, and scarlet anemones laughed their song of beauty. Poppies painted the smoother slopes bright red, embellished now and then by the blue of peablossoms. On some slopes the patchwork quilt of color was broken by the white of tiny ground-cover blossoms, brought to ephemeral life by the last rains. The sky was faintly blue, like polished turquoise.

The shepherd sat in the shadow of a great rock, his back against its rough surface. His head rested on his drawn-up knees and his folded arms. Beside him a long staff swung in the light touch of the vagrant breeze, its

smooth crook hooked over the twisted limb of a tall
juniper. He did not need to lift his head to watch the
sheep. They were scattered over the land at the base of
the hill, blending in color with the stones until it was hard
to tell them apart. Their movements were almost imper-
ceptible as they grazed. Tomorrow the ruddy-cheeked
shepherd lad would lead them over the hill where he now
sat and down to another valley where the grass was greener.

The shepherd sat contentedly. He was very young. No
down of coming beard had yet touched his face. While he
sat, great dreams sifted through his already poetic mind.
This was the sweetest time of all his years; something inside
him told him so. He would enjoy every blessed moment
of this peace. The dreams were at first as intangible as
wavering threads of gossamer, wafted by unfelt zephyrs.
Then the threads were larger, like those spun by a spider
with instinctive purpose, weaving a net, spreading it over
his heart to catch the dewdrop beauty of his dreams, holding them as the true web does its own watery pearls, glistening, blinking, in the rising sun.

At last the shepherd lifted his touseled head. His eyes
sought out the hills of Moab to the east, a ragged purple
line. At the foot of the hills, the sheen of the Dead Sea
separated part of Judea from Moab. All around him were
beauty and strength. The rocky hills were old. Some of
them towered into the sky. They spoke to his listening
heart of God. It was probably then, in a moment of rapture, that the shepherd boy murmured the opening words
of Psalm 121: "I will lift up mine eyes unto the hills, from
whence cometh my help.

* * *

I do not hold with the squeamish modern translators who thought that the words of David smacked of animism, and put a question where he had none: "If I lift up mine eyes to the hills, where shall I find help?" Perhaps, due to the lack of punctuation, the Hebrew will allow this, but *my own heart will not.*

Almost my whole life has been spent either in the mountains or in the shadow of them. I know how David felt; I know what he meant. Moreover, I think he said it the way the King James Version has it. He looked to the mountains, and they were the bulwark of his strength *because they reminded him of the God who made them.* He said in the very next breath, "My help cometh from the Lord, who made heaven and earth."

* * *

My memory spins back through sixty years. Dad and I had been down to Hitchcock's store. That is in the Little Ozarks. It is still there . . . .

Five years ago my wife and I visited the rustic building, sacred to my memory. I introduced myself to the little woman behind the counter—Mrs. Hitchcock, a widow now—and she said, "You are Harve Dye's boy. I know." It had been fifty-five years since she had seen either my dad or me! Life means something to mountain people. . . .

On the top of the mountain above Hitchcock's store Dad ran a trading post for the Indians. He spoke Cherokee as well as he did English.

On this night so long ago, Dad bought a knife and chain for me in Hitchcock's marvelous establishment, where you could buy anything from a toothpick to a wagon tongue, from a garden hoe to a gang plow. Today it sells gasoline and government bonds, shotgun shells and DDT.

We started up the wagon road, climbing up the mountain after dark. The Lord spills darkness down in the Ozarks like black paint out of a bucket.

I stumbled along on wobbly little legs with aching eyes trying to see the sapling stumps and flinty rocks before I smashed my toes against them. The more I looked, the less I saw. Finally I just gave up and let Dad be for me what Hobab was for the children of Israel—eyes in the wilderness. I held his hand.

After what seemed an eternity of darkness we saw the lights of home shining at the end of the rough old road. My heart thumped with joy. It was then, and only then, that I put my question to Dad:

"Daddy, how do you walk through the dark without falling down like I do?"

My father stopped short. I could feel him looking down at me with those serious gray eyes.

"It's this way, Sonny Boy. You stumble because you keep looking down. You are trying to see your own feet." Then taking my head in his hands, Dad pointed my eyes upward. "Look up there. Do you see where the sky is lighter? That's because the trees have been cut out to make the road. I have walked looking up there." And with an inspiration for which I have blessed him these long years, my wise Christian father said: "And that's a lesson for life, Son. Keep looking up."

The way today is dark. Uncertainty and fear cover our path. But we can walk without stumbling, and in complete confidence, if we keep looking up.

* * *

Since this has been a most personal book, intentionally designed that way, let me share another experience which enriched my life.

The sun bounced for one breathless moment on the rim of the ten-thousand-foot-high Sacramentos and then rolled down the other side, leaving the high rimrock on which I stood gently swathed in the filmy nightgown of the gathering dusk.

The chill of the fall evening crept through my leather jacket and on into my vitals as I leaned my high-powered rifle against a stump and blew warm breath on slightly numbed fingers. I glanced backward over the cedar-dotted mesa to where three horsemen rode stolidly my way, their mounts gingerly picking paths through the jagged rocks with heads bent to loosened reins. As they drew nearer, I saw the carcass of a huge muley buck draped across the saddle of the dun mare. A New Mexico rancher, Joseph Miller, rode triumphantly on her rump. His grin was wide as the riders drew near, their horses' hooves kicking up little sprays of dust.

"You oughta been on your way back to the ranch," Joseph said, chidingly, after I had expressed due admiration of his trophy.

"Just one teeny-weeny problem," I replied. "Where is the ranch?"

Joseph let off a loud guffaw, which startled a blue jay into angry rejoinder. It cocked its tufted head in feathery indignation from a swaying cedar branch and expressed its uninhibited opinion of us in unladylike terms. Joseph yelled, "Aw, shut up, you miserable camp robber!" Then, to me, "Don't tell me that a great hunter has done gone and got hisself lost!" His sarcasm was playful.

"I am not lost," I answered stiffly. "I am right here—"

"But the ranch done got itself lost. Is that what you
were going to say?" The rancher finished my sentence
and punctuated it with another bellowing laugh. This
was too much for the blue jay, and it took to its wings
with one last protesting squawk. My host beckoned to
me. "Come here and I'll show you the ranch right before your eyes."

I went over and stood by his horse's neck, my eyes
following his calloused finger, pointed like a revolver at
a distant target.

"Do you see that white splotch down there in the flat?
It is about four miles away. That is my pasture with the
horse corral just beyond. Then, right on back of that a
couple of hundred yards in that black spot which you can
barely see is the ranch house. Now you be careful. It's
pretty rough going between here and there, and I don't
want you falling down and breaking a leg. We'd just have
to shoot you."

Then they were gone, and I stood on what seemed to
be the rocky rim of the world. The prickly fingers of
dread began to pluck at my heart. How would I ever find
my way down there? I wanted to run after the horsemen.
Darkness was coming on with just a bare whisper of warn-
ing. The New Mexico mountains know no twilight. Once
darkness had enfolded the hills, the white blotch would be
no more. Besides, there were intervening ridges between
where I stood and the house; and, even if the light lingered
a little longer, my vision would soon be blocked. I prayed—
and I am afraid that some of my most fervent prayers have

been at times like that.

Then I saw it! My eyes had instinctively sought the heavens as though in search of God, and I saw a blazing torch in his hand. The planet Venus had danced out from behind the velvet curtain of the sky in all her glory as the evening star. Far below, seemingly directly under her scintillating feet, the white blotch which was my landmark faded out of sight. It made no difference. I knew then that I could find my way. All that I had to do was to keep looking up, now and then, to the bright, shining planet and eventually I would find my way back to the ranch house.

I picked up my rifle and started on my hazardous way. Before I had traveled three hundred yards, a ridge intervened and I had to work my way over it. I tripped over underbrush, and it caught at my clothing. Now and then some thorny bush jabbed at my legs. It was after ten o'clock before I neared the pasture. It was then that I saw a lantern bobbing, and soon I was hailed by Joseph Miller. I had made it safely.

When I think of this episode, buried in my past, I am always reminded of the words of Jesus: "I am . . . the bright and morning star."

For, you see, the planet Venus is either the morning or the evening star, depending upon the season.

The lesson is clear. With our eyes fixed upon Jesus, we can always find our way. He is the Light which lights the path of everyone with spiritual eyes to see.

Speaking of that Light:

He was just a lonely sheep herder on a bleak New Mexico desert. I came upon him late in the afternoon and saw him

standing there slim and straight, facing the sunset. He
was in an attitude of prayer, quiet and still.

The sheep had rolled themselves into gray balls and
looked like granite boulders on the hillside. A staccato
chatter of blue quail was borne on the evening breeze
as they made down for the night.

Here was peace.

I felt it stealing into my own soul as I faced the sunset
with the one to whom I had not yet spoken. I felt that
he was my brother though his skin was red, and he would
undoubtedly speak with a strange Indian dialect when I
finally broke the silence.

We stood for a moment of worship together as God
threw a gorgeous picture against the backdrop of a flaming
sky. It was a picture wildly beautiful, shouting for all to
hear and make no mistake about it: "I, who move before
your eyes, am the Lord God Almighty. Take the shoes
from off your feet, for the place where you stand is holy
ground."

We worshiped together, the stranger and I, and we were
strangers no longer.

Three thousand miles away I came upon another man.
He stood on the frozen Alaskan tundra far above the Arctic
Circle. The wolf fur of his parka framed his round face as
with a halo, though it was midnight. He had seen the
miracle hundreds of times before, though I had not seen
it once. Together we bowed before the glory of the Lord
as it shone in the light of the Aurora Borealis.

We spoke no word but watched while God hung the
shimmering, gossamer curtains across the sable canopy of
a freezing sky. Unlike the flamboyant coloring of a western

sunset, the northern lights were quietly pastel. They
were always moving: fading, undulating, wavering, ad-
vancing, retreating, never still but for a moment. Far
to our left the moon nestled in a crotch of the mountains.
Like an old-fashioned portiere button it seemed to clasp
a filmy, rippling, faintly iridescent drapery which tied
the shadowy mountain to the luminous sky and un-
folded, as we watched, across the heavens above the
lonely, winding Steese Highway to the faraway crown
of another gigantic mountain to our right. The coverlet
of starlit velvet above our heads was cut completely in
half by the flickering band of variegated light. Through
some strange, supernal artistry, God had changed the
wildly jagged mountains into a holy temple and the glory
of his train filled it.

There was no command to the Eskimo or to me to
worship; we could not help it. As though the still small
voice which so intrigued the prophet Elijah had spoken
to our hearts as well, we listened while God whispered
of his beauty to our souls.

Here, as on the desert of New Mexico, was a place of
prayer.

The psalmist was right when he cried out of the full-
ness of a reverent heart: "The heavens declare the glory
of God; and the firmament showeth his handiwork."

Forty-nine years ago I stood looking into the depths
of luminous eyes turned up to mine. In those beautiful
eyes I read an old, old story—old as the Garden of Eden.
They were the eyes of my bride, and in them I saw great
love—love which I did not deserve and did not understand,
then or now—but a love which I gratefully accepted and

returned with the hope that I would be worthy of it.

Then, one mystic day, I saw the light of love in the eyes of our firstborn—a curly-haired baby girl. She looked up at me with a trust which I have never betrayed.

The glory of life is love—a candle lighting the soul toward that more perfect day.

The flaming skies of a western sunset lead the devout soul close to God who painted them; the moving curtains of the Aurora Borealis swirl about his throne; the light in the eyes of wife or child lead just a little closer—but—

We finally arrive when we look up into the face of him who is the Savior of the world, Jesus, Son of God, and Lord of our own hearts.

He is the Light of the World; he is God's glory; he is God! We lift up our eyes today and see him, not dead and broken on a wooden cross on a blood spattered hill called Golgotha, but we see him on the throne of heaven:

"And there shall be no night there; and they need no candle, neither light of the sun; for the Lord God giveth them light: and they shall reign forever and forever"— so wrote the seer of Patmos.

This little book has not dealt with death—being concerned only with life, and that more abundantly in its fading years upon the earth.

Now that we near that greatest of all adventures of the soul, let us look at torches held in the hands of two old prophets. The first is Amos. Listen to him: "Seek him that maketh the seven stars (the Pleiades) and Orion, and turneth the shadow of death into morning" (Amos 5:8). The last great shadow will be lifted by the light of that eternal day.

And the gentle Zechariah: "But it shall be one day which shall be known to the Lord, not day, nor night: but it shall come to pass that at evening time it shall be light" (Zech. 14:7).

And the shepherd lad, now grown old, looked up into the face of another Shepherd and whispered, "Yea, though I walk through the valley of the shadow of death, I will fear no evil: for thou art with me; thy rod and thy staff they comfort me."

Through the valley. No dead-end street here. No cul-de-sac. No box canyon. No! A thoroughfare—a through street—quickly through the gathering darkness into ineffable light.

Look UP!